MEDITERRANEAN I
Quick and Easy
Everyday Cookbook

165+ Fast, Flavorful Recipes Ready In 30 Minutes or Less with Simple Ingredients and a 60-Day Meal Plan for Lasting Health

Maria Giordano

Copyright © 2025 by Maria Giordano

All rights reserved. The content contained within this book may not be reproduced, duplicated or transmitted without direct written permission from the author or the publisher. Under no circumstances will any blame or legal responsibility be held against the publisher, or author, for any damages, reparation, or monetary loss due to the information contained within this book, either directly or indirectly.

Legal Notice:

This book is copyright protected. It is only for personal use. You cannot amend, distribute, sell, use, quote or paraphrase any part, or the content within this book, without the consent of the author or publisher.

Disclaimer Notice

Please note the information contained within this document is for educational and entertainment purposes only. All effort has been executed to present accurate, up to date, reliable, complete information. No warranties of any kind are declared or implied. Readers acknowledge that the author is not engaging in the rendering of legal, financial, medical or professional advice. The content within this book has been derived from various sources. Please consult a licensed professional before attempting any techniques outlined in this book.

By reading this document, the reader agrees that under no circumstances is the author responsible for any losses, direct or indirect, that are incurred as a result of the use of information contained within this document, including, but not limited to, errors, omissions, or inaccuracies.

Table of Contents

INTRODUCTION 5
   Why Choose The Mediterranean Diet? 5
   Health Benefits Of The Mediterranean Diet 7
   Foods To Eat 8
   Daily Food Options 8
   Foods To Be Eaten 3-5 Times Weekly 8
   Foods to eat 2-3 times Weekly 8
   Foods To Limit or Avoid 9
   The Mediterranean Principles Of Nutrition 9
   The Mediterranean Food Pyramid 10
MEDITERRANEAN DIET RECIPES 11
   BREAKFAST RECIPES 11
      Date and Nut Granola with Greek Yogurt 11
      Mediterranean Breakfast Sandwich 12
      Herb & Feta Savory Muffins 12
      Vegetable Omelet 13
      Pan Con Tomate 14
      Green Poached Eggs on Toast 14
      Buckwheat Pancakes with Coconut Cream 15
      Apricot and Almond Breakfast CousCous 16
      Greek Omelette with Mint and Zucchini 16
      Mediterranean Chickpea and Spinach Breakfast Bowl 17
      Shakshuka 18
      Avocado Toast with Caramelized Balsamic Onions 18
      Sweet Potato Hash 19
      Tuna and White Bean Salad with Poached Eggs. 20
      Parmesan & Spinach Egg Bake 20
      Mint Tea and Olive Biscuits 21
      Eggs Florentine 22
      Lebanese Breakfast Bulgur Cereal with Fruit and nuts 22
      Turkish Breakfast Wrap with Sausage, Eggs and Vegetables 23
      Mediterranean Breakfast Pita 24
      Cauliflower Tabbouleh 24
      Busy Morning Egg Muffins 25
      Lemon-Dill Asparagus 26
      Tomato Toasts with Mint Yogurt and Sumac Vinaigrette 26
      Fried Eggs with Smoked Salmon and Lemon Cream 27
   MEDITERRANEAN LUNCH RECIPES 28
      Mussels with Cheese 28
      Meal-Prep Falafel Bowls with Tahini Sauce 28
      Chinese Cabbage with Mint and Green Peas 29
      Crispy Smoked Tofu & Coleslaw Wraps 30
      Scallop Ceviche 30
      Salmon Rice Bowl 31
      Chicken with Tomatoes, Prunes, Cinnamon, and Wine 32
      Organic Mini Minty Lamb Koftas 32
      Chicken Fajita Soup 33
      Grenadian Cod and Orange Salad with Olives 34
      Baked Prawns with Tomatoes and Feta 35
      Ben Tish's Duck and Fig Ponchos 35
      Linguine with Sun-dried Tomatoes. Olives, and Lemon 36
   MEDITERRANEAN DINNER RECIPES 38
      Spinach Ravioli with Artichokes & Olives 38
      Feta & Roasted Red Pepper Stuffed Chicken Breast 38
      Walnut-Rosemary Crusted Salmon 39
      Padma Lakshmi's Tandoori Chicken Salad 40
      Asparagus Risotto 41
      One-Skillet salmon with Fennel & Sun-dried Tomato Couscous 41
      BBQ Shrimp with Garlicky Kale & Parmesan-Herb Couscous 42
      Seafood Ravioli in Cream Cheese Sauce 43
      One Pot Beef Stew 44
      Linguine with Creamy White Clam Sauce 45
      Bean Counter Chowder 45
      Chicken Adobo 46
      Moroccan Chicken Pastilla 47
      One-Pan Chicken Parmesan Pasta 48
      Creamy Seafood Bisque 49
      Tomato and Pepper Poached Cod 49
      Tahini Chicken with Polenta 50
      Spanish Grilled Sardines With Lemon, Garlic, and Paprika 51
      Baked Haddock with Baby Bell Peppers 52
      Red Lentil Soup Mix 53
   MEDITERRANEAN RICE AND PASTA DISHES 54
      Mediterranean Rice Pilaf 54
      Lemon-Garlic Shrimp Pasta 54
      Mushroom risotto 55
      Bruschetta Chicken Pasta 56
      Maqbouleh 57
      One-Pot Tomato Basil Pasta 57
      Turkish pilaf 58
      Passion Fruit and Spicy Couscous 59
      Cauliflower Rice Paella 59
      Farfalle with Tuna, Lemon, and Fennel 60
      Spanakorizo 61
      Seared Salmon with Pesto Fettuccine 61
      Risotto Carbonara 62
      Spaghetti Al Pomodoro Crudo 63
      Risi e Bisi (Venetian-style rice and peas) 63
      Pasta with Arugula and Walnut Pesto 64
      Garlic & Seafood Couscous 64
      Mediterranean-Style Chicken and Rice 65
      Feta and Tomato Rice 66
      Tomato and Cherry Linguine 66
   MEDITERRANEAN SNACKS RECIPES 68
      Spicy Rosemary Olives 68
      Rosemary-Garlic Pecans 68

- Salmon Cakes with Potato and Fire Roasted Corn Salsa 69
- Carrot Cake Energy Bites 69
- Pistachio & Peach Toast 70
- Spanakopita 70
- Tuna Deviled Eggs 71
- French Tuna Rillettes 72
- Peanut Butter Sesame Seed Balls 72
- Greek Yogurt Breakfast Parfait 73
- White Corn Balls 73
- Muhammara (Roasted Red Pepper and Walnut Dip) 74
- Tortilla De Patata (Spanish Potato Omelets) .. 74
- Crunchy Granola 75
- Savory Date & Pistachio Bites 76
- Zucchini Fritters with Feta, Cheddar, Mint and Parsley 76
- Kalamata Olive Tapenade 77
- Greek Salad Skewers 77
- Everything-Bagel Crispy Chickpeas 78
- Apple with Cinnamon Almond Butter 79
- Peanut Butter Energy Balls 79
- Greek Fava 79
- Almond Crackers 80
- Kale Chips 81
- Classic Hummus with Pita Bread 81
- Greek Stuffed Grape Leaves 82

MEDITERRANEAN SOUP RECIPES 84
- White Bean Soup with Escarole 84
- Chicken Meatball Soup 84
- Greek Bean Soup (Fasolada) 85
- Seafood Soup 86
- Italian White Bean Soup 87
- Lemony Greek Chickpea Soup 88
- Arborio Rice and White Bean Soup 88
- Pea Stew 89
- Summer Squash & White Bean Soup 90
- Eggplant Stew 90
- Chicken Spinach Soup with Fresh Pesto 91
- Jackfruit And Chili Stew 92
- Vegetable Ravioli Soup 92

MEDITERRANEAN SALADS RECIPES 94
- Mediterranean Edamame & Herb Salad 94
- Balela Salad 94
- Greek Pasta Salad 95
- Mediterranean Chickpea Egg Salad 96
- Pesto Pasta Salad 97
- Cannellini Bean Lettuce Wraps 97
- Chicken Edamame Salad 98
- Leafy Lacinato Tuscan Treat 99
- Feta & Black Bean Salad 99
- Goat Cheese and Red Beans Salad 100
- 15-Minute Mediterranean Sardine Salad 100
- Tomato Slices with Feta Cheese and Fresh Herbs 101

MEDITERRANEAN DESSERTS RECIPES 103
- Blueberry Cake 103
- Blackberry and Apple Cobbler 103
- Orange and Apricots Cake 104
- Blueberry Yogurt Mousse 104
- Loukoumades (Fried Honey Balls) 105
- Cottage Cheese Mousse & Berries 105
- Almond Peaches Mix 106
- Cocoa Brownies 106
- Mixed Berries Stew 107
- Almond and Oats Pudding 107
- Banana Cinnamon Cupcakes 108
- Creamy Mint Strawberry Mix 108
- Cinnamon Chickpeas Cookies 109
- Mango Bowls 109

MEDITERRANEAN VEGETARIAN DISHES 110
- Spanish Rice and Beans 110
- Broccoli and Lentil Cakes with Avocado 111
- Healthy Basil Platter 111
- Onion Pakora 112
- Farinata 113
- Curried Cashews 113
- Batata Harra 114

MEDITERRANEAN MEAT RECIPES 116
- Grilled Turmeric Chicken 116
- Grilled Chicken and Hummus in Pita 116
- Yogurt-Marinated Chicken 117
- Spiced Lamb Chops 118
- Chicken in a Caper Sauce 119
- Ground Turkey Skillet Dinner with Spinach, Tomatoes, White Beans and Homemade Croutons 119

MEDITERRANEAN FISH AND SEAFOOD DISHES 121
- Pan Seared Shrimp with Lemon-Garlic Braised Greens 121
- Shrimp Scampi 122
- Tilapia & Capers 122
- Italian Seafood Risotto with Saffron and Prawns 123
- Stewed Squid 124
- Trout & Wilted Greens 124

60-DAYS MEDITERRANEAN DIET MEAL PLAN 126

INTRODUCTION

The Mediterranean diet stands out as one of the healthiest diets in the world. It remains one of the most effective diets for weight loss, improving cardiovascular health, and reducing the aging process. In addition to this, the people of the Mediterranean area are also renowned for their higher life expectancy, healthy skin, and great figures. In this book, you'll learn about the benefits of the Mediterranean diet, foods to consume and avoid, and, most importantly, over 165 flavorful recipes you can make in less than 30 Minutes.

Let's begin by first understanding what the Mediterranean diet is about. This unique diet has its roots from Greece, Spain, France up to the Mediterranean Sea. However, with the variety of cultures it originates from, the Mediterranean diet maintains a consistency across these cultures: it is a plant-rich diet. Plant-rich because it is mainly plant-based, it does not exclude animal-based ingredients. The dishes are usually rich in omega-3 fatty acids, healthy fats as well as fiber.

Red Meat, sugary foods, processed foods, and most dairy, save for yogurt and cheese, are largely limited or avoided altogether in this diet. This means your classic Mediterranean dish has its main ingredient, which is a variety of vegetables served with healthy proteins like chicken on the side. The major source of healthy fats is olive oil.

Focusing on using a variety of herbs such as oregano, garlic, thyme, basil, and rosemary, this diet encourages a reduced usage of salt and artificial seasonings for your food. Your cooking and eating choices aren't the only change that comes with the diet; your drinking choices are also a part of the diet. A small serving of a glass of wine is recommended within the diet, but it cannot be taken beyond that small serving on a daily basis. Honey and fresh fruits are used to satisfy sweet cravings. You'll quickly come to realize that the Mediterranean diet targets your entire eating pattern, creating healthy dish alternatives without complicating it with strict calculations to stick to.

Why Choose The Mediterranean Diet?

It is important to note that the Mediterranean diet might not be an easy palate to get used to because of its very natural food choices and eating patterns. However, it accounts for this with various dishes across cultures to choose from. Here are some reasons to make the switch to this diet plan.

1. The Environmental Sustainability of the Diet: At the core of the Mediterranean diet, you have fruits, vegetables, nuts, and basically plant-based dishes. Ingredients are used entirely, from the stems to the leaves, even peels. This creates no room for food waste, as well as a reduction in the overall impact of food production on the environment. Animal-

based products generally have a higher environmental impact compared to plant-based diets.

The diet type also encourages various practices that align with eco-friendly and responsible food choices. Emphasizing the use of locally sourced ingredients and seasonal ingredients reduces the need for long-distance transportation. Carbon emissions associated with food distribution are also largely cut down.

2. Mindful Eating: Portion control is a crucial part of the Mediterranean diet. It ensures mindful eating by being aware of portion sizes. This can be especially useful if you're on a weight loss journey or are more conscious of your food size intake. The Mediterranean diet encourages individuals to pay attention to their hunger, craving, and fullness cues. When you're in tune with your body's needs, you can better handle overeating and regulate your food intake.

    Mindful eating also shows up in the intentionality behind the dish choices. Choosing fresh, seasonal, and locally sourced ingredients shows intentionality and mindful eating. Eating is unhurried, allowing proper mastication, which slows down appetite and leaves room to enjoy the full taste of each bite thoroughly.

3. Exploration of the Mediterranean cultures: The Mediterranean diet allows you a view/experience of the Mediterranean cultures through their food. For adventurous people, this could be a treat! The Mediterranean diet goes back thousands of years to ancient civilizations such as Greece and Rome. It carries the culinary legacy of these ancient societies to date, which valued the use of fresh and local ingredients and their dietary evolutions.

4. Delicious, Savory nature of the diet: You'll find that Mediterranean cuisine is quite particular with its preference for fresh herbs and spices for enhancing your food flavor. Basil, thyme, mint, garlic, and oregano will easily become your go-to choices for infusing your dishes with aromatic and savory notes. On exploring savory Mediterranean dishes, Mediterranean cultures embrace the concept of "mezze" and "tapas," which are a variety of small, flavorful dishes served on small plates alongside the main dishes.

    The vast options for seafood, legumes, whole grains, and fruits from the different Mediterranean cultures create room to choose delicious dishes from. External influences on Mediterranean cuisine, also enrich the dish choices and eating experiences.

Health Benefits Of The Mediterranean Diet

The major highlight of the Mediterranean diet is its health benefits. Due to the fresh nature of all ingredients of the Mediterranean diet, each Mediterranean dish is doused with a ton of benefits. Each dish is nutrient-dense and a good option for health-conscious consumers.

Let's check out some of these benefits:

1. Increased Cardiovascular health and minimal risk of heart diseases: The Mediterranean diet is associated with reduced risk of heart disease due to olive oil being the major source of healthy fats. Olive oil contains sufficient monosaturated fats, which help lower bad/high cholesterol levels. There are also fatty fish like salmon, sardines, and mackerel, which are nutrient-dense in omega-3 fatty acids.

   These fats have anti-inflammatory properties, help prevent atherosclerosis (hardening of the arteries) and reduce triglycerides. The high fiber content from the diet can lower blood pressure and improve blood vessel function. Resveratrol, an antioxidant present in red wine, contributes to overall heart health as well.

2. Improved Digestion: This one's a no-brainer! The diverse amount of nuts, fruits, whole grains, vegetables, and legumes account for a high fiber content, which is super helpful in digestion. The fiber-rich dishes promote regular bowel movement and a healthy gut microbiome and prevent constipation. With a balanced gut microbiome, you can reduce the risk of gastrointestinal disorders. Mindful eating also reduces the chances of overeating, which could lead to indigestion and digestive discomfort.

   The diet's avoidance of high-fat foods and heavily processed food items can help reduce the risk of developing or exacerbating any symptoms of IBS (Irritable Bowel Syndrome).

3. Enhanced Mood and Health: Studies have shown that following the Mediterranean diet might impact mental health positively. Dishes rich in omega-3 fatty acids, antioxidants, and whole foods, all found in the Mediterranean diet, support brain function and mood regulation. Whole grains also help stabilize blood glucose levels. When the blood glucose levels are balanced, it allows for maintaining a stable mood and energy levels throughout the day.

4. Weight management: The Mediterranean diet is largely effective for weight loss. Its focus on whole vegetables, portion control, and minimally processed foods is a safe regimen for

weight management. Abundant in fiber from fruits, legumes, whole grains, and vegetables enhances feelings of fullness and delays gastric emptying. This helps in controlling hunger and reducing overall calorie intake.

The fiber-high and nutrient-dense nature of Mediterranean foods gives you minerals and vitamins whilst keeping you in a calorie deficit for losing weight.

Foods To Eat

Following the Mediterranean diet requires knowing the right foods to eat. A good pictorial representation of the diet is illustrated on the Mediterranean diet pyramid. However, here are the food items you can consume under the Mediterranean diet:

Daily Food Options

This involves food items you can incorporate into your daily feeding. This means Whole grains, fruits, legumes, nuts, olive oil, seeds, nuts, herbs and spices.

- Whole Grains include barley, couscous, oats, bulgur, farro, buckwheat, quinoa, whole-grain bread, wheat
- Fruits include Apples, Apricots, Berries, bananas, cantaloupes, cherries, dates, figs, grapes, oranges, pomegranates, pears, peaches, papaya, and many others.
- Nuts and Seeds: Walnuts, almonds, sunflower seeds, cashew nuts, and many other nuts and seeds.
- Legumes: Sesame seeds, peanuts, beans, and many others.
- Herbs and Spices: These include pepper, garlic, rosemary, ginger, cinnamon, ginger, rosemary, mint, parsley, basil, sage, thyme and so much more. Ensure to experiment with these to find out which best complements your dishes.

Foods To Be Eaten 3-5 Times Weekly

These are foods to be eaten 3-5 times a week. This tier contains primarily fish and seafood.

- Oily Fish: These are fishes rich in omega-3 fatty acids. Examples include salmon, mackerel, sardines, albacore tuna, trout and anchovies.
- Lean Fish: Halibut, bass, Cod, tilapia, haddock, and grouper.
- Seafood: Mussels, lobster, shrimps, periwinkles, crab, clams and calamari

Foods to eat 2-3 times Weekly

These are foods to eat in meticulous portions at most 3 times weekly. This has majorly other animal-based proteins.

- Poultry: Turkey, duck, chicken, and quail are excellent lean protein sources. They provide essential amino acids and are a valuable addition to meals.
- Eggs, Sour Cream, Fatty Yogurt, and Cheese as well. Be careful when making cheese choices not to pick highly processed cheese.

Foods To Limit or Avoid

The foods below are a no-no or should be taken sparsely in minute quantities in the Mediterranean diet.

- Sweets: These include sugary treats, candies, and ice-cream
- Red Meat
- Fast food
- Refined Cereal
- Foods with Saturated fats.

The Mediterranean Principles Of Nutrition

To ensure you get well acquainted with the workings of the Mediterranean diet, here are some tips to follow:

1. Eat whole grains at each meal. You can choose from brown rice, oats, or barley. Whatever you're feeling that day.
2. Eat a variety of fruits at/after each meal.
3. Vegetables and meat are steamed, baked, and grilled, not fried.
4. All cooking oils should be switched to olive oil.
5. All products must be fresh and should be consumed raw, if possible.
6. Incorporate different colors of vegetables into your dishes to spice them up.
7. Drink at least 1.5-2 liters of water daily.
8. Roast, sauté, and steam your vegetables for a change of taste and flavor. You can also make them into soups.
9. Use low-fat milk and dairy alternatives such as kefir and yogurt.
10. Be experimental with your spices to increase your appetite.
11. Eat at least two servings of seafood and 2-4 eggs weekly.
12. Take wine, but in moderate quantities, with your meals.

The Mediterranean Food Pyramid

This is a graphical representation of the Mediterranean diet created to better understand the eating structure. The pyramid shows the different food groups in "tiers," showing the consumption amount and weekly frequency.

At the base of the pyramid, you find the Mediterranean lifestyle and habits to incorporate as you commit to the diet such as communal eating, physical activities, etc.

The first tier follows the base and shows the foods to be consumed regularly. This includes all plant-based foods.

Following the first tier is the second tier, which illustrates that food should be consumed just twice within a week. The food items within this tear include fish and seafood. This means that fish- or seafood-based dishes be taken twice a week.

The third tier identifies the foods that should be eaten as sides in complete moderation daily to weekly. This includes eggs, cheese, poultry, and yogurt.

On the final tier, we see foods to avoid or take in tiny quantities. Foods like red meat or containing saturated fat should be skipped or substituted when possible.

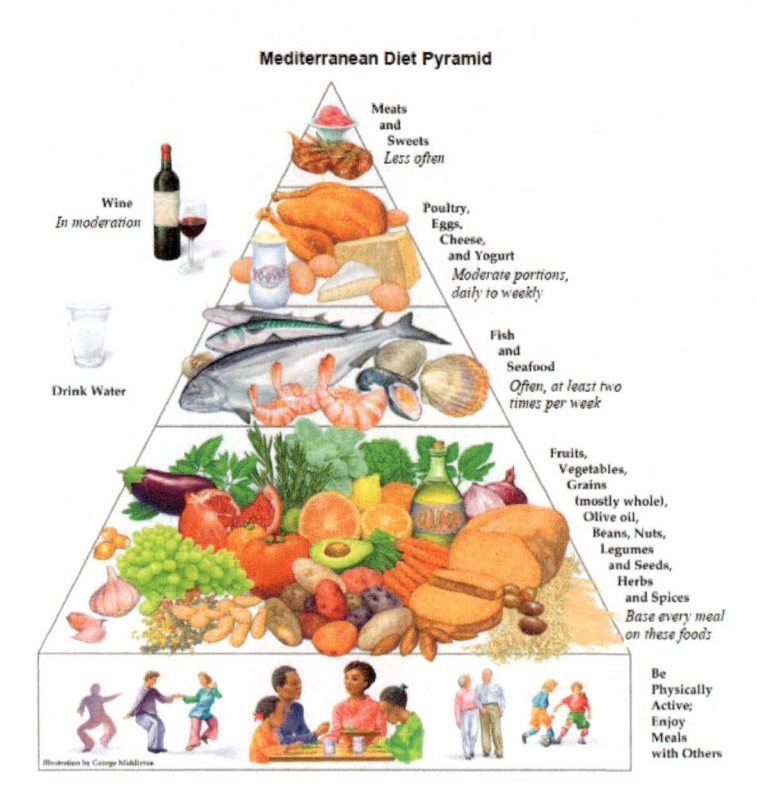

The Mediterranean Diet Pyramid

MEDITERRANEAN DIET RECIPES

BREAKFAST RECIPES

Date and Nut Granola with Greek Yogurt

Prep: 10 minutes | Cook: 25 minutes | Serves 2

Ingredients:

- Rolled Oats
- 50g dried dates, chopped
- Walnuts, chopped
- Almonds, chopped
- 2 tbsp honey
- 2 tbsp chia seeds
- 2 tbsp coconut oil, melted
- Greek Yogurt
- ½ tsp vanilla extract
- Fresh berries for topping

Instructions:

1. Preheat oven to 165ºC and line the baking sheet with parchment paper.
2. Combine chopped walnuts, almonds, chia seeds, and rolled oats in a bowl.
3. Whisk some honey, melted coconut oil, and vanilla extract in a separate bowl.
4. Pour the wet mixture onto the dry mixture and mix into each other until the dry mixture is well coated.
5. Pour the mixture on the prepared baking sheet and spread evenly. Bake this for 20-25 minutes, stirring it in intervals to ensure even cooking.
6. Cook until golden brown.
7. Take it out of the oven and let it cool. Once cooled, mix in the chopped dried dates.
8. Serve your Granola with Greek yogurt and toppings.

Nutritional Facts (Per Serving): Calories: 400 | Fat: 24g | Carbs: 40g | Fiber: 7g | Protein: 9g

Mediterranean Breakfast Sandwich

Prep: 10 minutes | Cook: 5 minutes | Serves 2

Ingredients:

- 4 slices whole-grain bread (toasted)
- 1 medium ripe avocado (mashed)
- 1 medium tomato (sliced)
- 2 large eggs
- 4 medium fresh lettuce leaves
- 2 tsp. olive oil
- Salt and pepper
- Red pepper flakes
- pinch of smoked paprika

Instructions:

1. Toast the bread slices until golden and crispy, and fry your eggs to your liking. Mash the ripe Avocado in a small bowl. Add salt and pepper to taste. Slice the tomato and get the hummus ready.
2. Spread the hummus evenly over each slice of toasted bread.
3. Layer each slice with fresh lettuce, tomato slices, and mashed avocado. Add a fried egg to each and top with the remaining toasted bread slices.
4. Slice the sandwiches in half for easier eating. Optionally, sprinkle red pepper flakes or smoked paprika for an extra kick.

Nutritional Facts Per Serving: Calories: 553 | Fat: 35g | Carbs: 41g | Fiber: 13g | Protein: 24g

Herb & Feta Savory Muffins

Prep: 15 minutes | Cook: 20 minutes | Serves 2

Ingredients:

- All-purpose flour
- ½ tsp baking soda
- 1 tsp baking powder
- ¼ tsp salt
- ¼ cup each, fresh herbs (parsley, dill, chives), chopped
- 1 egg
- Feta cheese (crumbled)
- Buttermilk
- Olive Oil

Instructions:

1. Heat the oven to 190°C and line a muffin tin with paper liners.
2. Mix the flour, salt, baking soda, and baking powder into a bowl and whisk together.
3. Stir the chopped herbs and the crumbled feta cheese into the dry flour mixture.
4. Beat the eggs in a separate bowl and add in the olive oil and buttermilk. Mix this well.
5. Mix the wet ingredients into the dry ingredients and gently fold until well combined.
6. Measure the batter into the muffin cups.
7. Bake this for 18-20 minutes or until a toothpick inserted into the muffin center comes out clean.
8. Allow the muffins cool slightly before serving.

Nutritional Facts (Per Serving): Calories: 380 | Fat: 38g | Carbs: 38g | Fiber: 1g | Protein: 10g

Vegetable Omelet

Prep: 2 minutes | Cook: 25 minutes | Serves 4

Ingredients:

- ½ cup diced tomatoes
- ½ cup cucumber
- ½ cup yellow squash
- ½ Avocado, ripe and chopped
- 2 eggs
- 2 tbsp, water
- 1 cup frozen egg product, thawed
- 1 tsp dried basil, crushed
- ¼ tsp ground black pepper
- ¼ tsp salt
- ¼ cup Monterey Jack cheese, shredded
- 1 fresh chive, snipped

Instructions:

1. Combine the tomatoes, squash, avocado, and cucumber in a medium-sized bowl and set aside.
2. In another medium bowl, whisk together the egg product, eggs, water, salt, basil, and pepper.
3. Coat a non-stick skillet generously with cooking spray. Heat the skillet over medium heat. Repeat this for each omelet.
4. Pour the egg into the heated skillet.
5. Immediately stir the eggs gently with a wooden spatula. Do this until the middle of the eggs looks cooked surrounded by liquid, then stop stirring.
6. Cook for 30-60 seconds until the egg is set.
7. Scoop the filling into one side of the omelet.

8. Fold the other side of the omelet over the filling. Take the omelet off the skillet and repeat until whisked eggs are finished.
9. Sprinkle some cheese over the omelet. Garnish with chives if desired.

Nutritional Facts (Per Serving): Calories:128 | Fat: 6g | Carbs: 7g | Protein: 12g

Pan Con Tomate

Prep: 10 minutes | Cook: 1 minute | Serves 4

Ingredients:

- ½ Baguette, cut into 1" sizes
- 1 clove garlic, crushed
- 1 medium ripe tomato
- 2 tbsp Extra-virgin olive oil
- Pinch of salt

Instructions:

1. Put the tomato, garlic, olive oil, and salt into a blender. Puree till smooth.
2. Toast the baguette slices in the oven or a toaster oven.
3. Drizzle a little olive oil on each cut bread piece and top the bread with a spoonful of tomato sauce.
4. Top with prosciutto, tuna or salmon.

Nutritional Facts (Per Serving): Calories: 153 | Fat: 8g | Carbs: 1g | Fiber: 1g | Protein: 3g

Green Poached Eggs on Toast

Prep: 5 minutes | Cook: 10 minutes | Serves 4

Ingredients:

- 4 Eggs
- 198g Smoked Salmon
- ½ Tsp Lemon Juice, Fresh
- 113g Avocado Flesh, Mashed
- 2 Tsp Soy Sauce
- 4 Bread Slices, Toasted
- Sea Salt & Black Pepper to Taste

Instructions:

1. Boil some water in a pot, stirring it to create a whirlpool.

2. Throw two eggs in, and allow it to cook. Continue for another two eggs.
3. Place all eggs in an ice bath to stop the cooking.
4. Scoop the flesh from your avocado and mash it. Put four toasted slices of bread on the serving plate, placing your avocado mash over them.
5. Top with smoked salmon, drizzling the lemon juice and soy sauce. Sprinkle with salt and pepper.
6. Top each one with a peeled, poached egg to serve.

Nutritional Facts (Per Serving): Calories: 460 | Fat: 30g | Carbs: 28g | Fiber: 5g | Protein: 30g

Buckwheat Pancakes with Coconut Cream

Prep: 10 minutes | Cook: 20 minutes | Serves 2

Ingredients:

- 2/3 cup buckwheat flour
- ¼ tsp baking soda
- 1 tsp baking powder
- ¼ tsp salt
- 1 egg
- ¾ cup almond or whole milk
- ¼ cup coconut cream
- 2 tsp maple syrup
- 1 tsp vanilla
- 4 tsp Extra-virgin olive oil

Topping:

- ½ cup full-fat syrup
- ¼ cup maple syrup

Instructions:

1. Mix all dry ingredients (buckwheat flour, baking soda, baking powder, and salt) in a bowl.
2. Inside another bowl, whisk the egg, almond milk, coconut cream, vanilla, and maple syrup.
3. Add the dry ingredients into the wet ingredients. Mix using a spoon but be careful not to overmix.
4. Fry the pancake mix in a pre-heated skillet with olive oil. Flip when bubbles show throughout the pancake.
5. Enjoy with yogurt and maple syrup.

Nutritional Facts (Per Serving):

Calories: 572 | Fat: 20g | Carbs: 90g | Fiber: 5g | Protein: 10g

Apricot and Almond Breakfast CousCous

Prep: 10 minutes | Cook: 10 minutes | Serves 2

Ingredients:

- Couscous
- Almonds, chopped
- Dried apricots, chopped
- 2 tbsp honey
- Water
- ½ tsp vanilla extract
- Greek yogurt

Instructions:

1. Bring 200ml of water to boil in a saucepan and take it off heat. Add the couscous, cover, and let it sit for 5 minutes.
2. Fluff the couscous with a fork and stir in the chopped almonds and dried apricots.
3. Drizzle some honey and vanilla extract over the couscous mixture, stirring to combine.
4. Serve the couscous in bowls, with some Greek yogurt as a topping.

Nutritional Facts (Per Serving): Calories: 350 | Fat: 7g | Carbs: 64g | Fiber: 6g | Protein: 9g

Greek Omelette with Mint and Zucchini

Prep: 5 minutes | Cook: 10 minutes | Serves 2

Ingredients:

- 1 large zucchini
- ¼ cup feta cheese
- 2 tbsp Extra-virgin olive oil
- 4 eggs
- 5 leaves fresh mint, chopped
- Salt and pepper to taste

Instructions:

1. Fry the zucchini slices (lightly salted) in olive oil until they're brown on both sides. Transfer them to a paper towel.

2. Whisk the eggs with some salt, pepper, and mint.
3. Heat up some of that reserved oil.
4. Pour in the eggs, then pour zucchini on one side of the eggs. Cover it with the other side and flip it to make an omelet. Serve with the Greek feta cheese.

Nutrition Facts (Per Serving): Calories: 333 | Fat: 27g | Carbs: 8g | Fiber: 2g | Protein: 16g

Mediterranean Chickpea and Spinach Breakfast Bowl

Prep: 10 minutes | Cook: 15 minutes | Serves 2

Ingredients:

- Baby Spinach
- Canned chickpeas, drained
- 2 large eggs
- 1 clove garlic, minced
- 1 tbsp olive oil
- ½ tsp ground cumin
- Salt and pepper to taste
- Kalamata olives
- Crumbled Feta Cheese
- Sun-dried Tomatoes

Instructions:

1. Preheat some olive oil in a skillet over medium heat. Pour in the minced garlic and cumin, sauteing for 1 minute.
2. Add in the chickpeas into the skillet and cook for 5-7 minutes until heated through.
3. Stir in the baby spinach and cook until it's wilted.
4. As the spinach wilts, fry the eggs to your preferred level of doneness in a pan.
5. Divide the chickpeas and spinach mixture between two bowls.
6. Add in some fried eggs, crumbled feta cheese, kalamata olives and sun-dried tomatoes into each bowl.

Nutritional Facts (Per Serving): Calories: 380 | Fat: 17g | Carbs: 37g | Fiber: 11g | Protein: 18g

Shakshuka

Prep: 15 minutes | Cook: 20 minutes | Serves 6

Ingredients:

- 2 tbsp olive oil
- 1 large onion, diced
- ½ cup sliced fresh mushrooms
- 1 tsp salt, plus more to taste
- 1 cup diced red bell pepper
- 1 jalapeño pepper, seeded and sliced
- 1 tsp cumin
- ½ tsp paprika
- ½ tsp ground turmeric
- ½ tsp freshly ground black pepper, plus more to taste
- ¼ tsp cayenne pepper
- 1 (794g) can crushed San Marzano tomatoes, or other high-quality plum tomatoes
- ½ cup water, or more as needed
- 6 large eggs
- 2 tbsp crumbled feta cheese
- 2 tbsp chopped fresh parsley

Instructions:

1. Heat olive oil in a pan. Stir in onion and mushrooms and season with salt. Cook until the mushrooms begin to brown, about 10 minutes.
2. Add in the tomatoes and water, reducing heat to simmer. Stir until the vegetables soften. Add more water if the sauce becomes too thick.
3. Make a large spoon to make a depression in sauce for each egg. Crack an egg into a small ramekin and slide gently into an indentation; repeat with remaining eggs. Season eggs with salt and pepper. Cover and cook until eggs reach desired doneness.

Nutritional Facts (Per Serving): Calories: 185 | Fat: 11g | Carbs: 16 | Fiber: 3g | Protein: 10g

Avocado Toast with Caramelized Balsamic Onions

Prep: 5 minutes | Cook: 20 minutes | Serves 2

Ingredients:

- 1 ripe Avocado
- 1 onion, sliced

- 2 slices toast
- 2 tbsp Extra-virgin olive oil
- 2tbsp Balsamic vinegar
- 1 tsp dried oregano
- Salt and pepper, to taste

Instructions:

1. Heat up the olive oil on medium heat. Add in the onions, salt and pepper. Sauté this for 20 minutes, stirring it regularly until it caramelizes.
2. Add the balsamic vinegar to the onions, cooking it for 2 minutes. Take this off the heat.
3. Mash the avocado, some oregano, salt, and pepper in a bowl using a fork until smooth.
4. Toast the 2 slices of bread, topping up each slice of the avocado mixture. Enjoy this with the caramelized onions.

Nutritional Facts (Per Serving): Calories: 388 | Fat: 30g | Carbs: 29g | Fiber: 9g | Protein: 5g

Sweet Potato Hash

Prep: 5 minutes | Cook: 25 minutes | Serves 3

Ingredients:

- ½ Tbsp Lemon Juice, Fresh
- ½ Tsp Honey, Raw
- Sea Salt & Black Pepper to Taste
- ½ Avocado, Peeled, Pit Removed & Diced
- 1 ½ Tbsp Olive Oil
- 1 Clove Garlic, Minced
- 1 Sweet Potato, Peeled & Cubed ½ Tbsp Apple Cider Vinegar
- 1/8 Cup Yellow Onion, Diced
- 225g Ham, Low Sodium & Diced
- 1/8 Cup Green Bell Pepper, Diced

Instructions:

1. Heat your oven to 165°C, then grease a baking sheet.
2. Season your sweet potatoes with salt and pepper before drizzling with half a tbsp of oil.
3. Arrange your potatoes on the baking sheet, baking for ten to fourteen minutes. They should be tender.
4. Combine your apple cider vinegar, garlic, a tbsp of oil, and honey together in a bowl. Whisk well.
5. Sauté until soft, and then add your ham into a skillet.
6. Cook until your meat is browned, and then mix your vinegar sauce, lemon juice, and avocado. Serve warm.

Nutritional Facts (Per Serving): Calories: 400 | Fat: 27g | Carbs: 23g | Fiber: 6g | Protein: 14g

Tuna and White Bean Salad with Poached Eggs

Prep: 15 minutes | Cook: 10 minutes | Serves 2

Ingredients:

- Canned white beans, rinsed
- Canned tuna, drained
- 4 large eggs, poached
- 160g cherry tomatoes, halved
- ½ red onion, finely chopped
- 2 tbsp olive oil
- 2 tbsp fresh parsley, chopped
- 1 tbsp red wine vinegar
- Salt and pepper to taste.

Instructions:

1. Combine white beans, canned tuna, cherry tomatoes, red onion, and fresh parsley in a large bowl.
2. In a smaller bowl, whisk together the olive oil, red wine vinegar, salt and pepper.
3. Pour the dressing on the salad and mix thoroughly.
4. Divide the salad into two plates, adding the poached eggs beside the salad.
5. Season the eggs with some more salt and pepper and serve immediately.

Nutrition Facts (Per Serving): Calories: 420 | Fat: 23g | Carbs: 26g | Fiber: 8g | Protein: 30g

Parmesan & Spinach Egg Bake

Prep: 10 minutes | Cook: 15 minutes | Serves 2

Ingredients:

- 1 Clove Garlic, Minced
- ½ Tomato, Small & Diced Fine
- ¼ Cup Parmesan Cheese, grated
- 2 Eggs
- 2 Cups Baby Spinach
- 1 Tsp Olive Oil

Instructions:

1. Start by turning your oven to 180°C, then get out an eight-inch casserole dish. Grease the dish and place it to the side.
2. Heat your oil in a skillet over medium heat. Once your oil is hot, add in your

spinach and garlic and cook for three minutes. Drain the skillet.
3. Add in your parmesan, and mix well. Place it in the casserole dish, then make two wells in the mixture. Crack an egg into each one.
4. Bake for fifteen minutes, and then remove it from the oven. Allow it to cool slightly before serving warm.

Nutritional Facts (Per Serving): Calories: 220 | Fat: 13g | Carbs: 6g | Fiber: 2g | Protein: 19g

Mint Tea and Olive Biscuits

Prep: 5 minutes | Cook: 10 minutes | Serves 2

Ingredients:

- 473 ml water
- 2 tsp green tea leaves
- 1 small bunch Fresh mint leaves
- 2 tsp honey
- 150g all-purpose flour
- 1 tsp baking powder
- ¼ tsp salt
- Olive oil
- Milk

Instructions:

1. Preheat the oven until 200°C and line a baking sheet using parchment paper.
2. Whisk the flour, baking powder, and salt together in a bowl.
3. Make a well in the center of the flour mixture and pour in the olive oil and milk.
4. Stir till it's well combined. Be careful not to overmix.
5. Turn out the dough, placing it on a floured surface, and pat gently into a 1-inch-thick circle.
6. Cut the dough into biscuit shapes using a biscuit cutter.
7. Bake for 8-10 minutes.
8. Bring 2 cups of water to a boil.
9. Place the green tea and mint leaves in a teapot.
10. Pour the boiling water over the tea leaves and let it steep for 3-5 minutes.
11. Sweeten the tea with honey, strain it, and serve it in teacups.
12. Serve the warm olive biscuits with the tea.

Nutritional Facts (Per Serving): Calories: 260 | Fat: 14g | Carbs: 30g | Fiber: 1g | Protein: 4g

Eggs Florentine

Prep: 10 minutes | Cook: 10 minutes | Serves 3

Ingredients:

- 2 tbsp unsalted butter
- ½ cup mushrooms, sliced
- 2 cloves garlic, minced
- ½ (283g) package fresh spinach
- 4 large eggs, slightly beaten
- salt and ground black pepper to taste
- 3 tbsp cream cheese, cut into small pieces

Instructions:

1. Melt butter in a large skillet over medium heat. Add mushrooms and garlic; cook and stir until garlic is fragrant, about 1 minute. Add spinach; cook until wilted, 2 to 3 minutes.
2. Stir in eggs; season with salt and pepper. Cook, without stirring, until eggs start to firm; flip. Sprinkle cream cheese over egg mixture; cook until cream cheese starts to soften, about 5 minutes.

Nutritional Facts (Per Serving): Calories: 279 | Fat: 23g | Carbs: 4g | Fiber: 1g | Protein: 16g

Lebanese Breakfast Bulgur Cereal with Fruit and nuts

Prep: 5 minutes | Cook: 15 minutes | Serves 2

Ingredients:

- 1 cup dry medium bulgur
- ½ cup milk of your choice (cow, almond, soy, etc.)
- Dried or fresh fruit
- 1 tbsp honey or maple syrup
- ¼ cup almonds or walnuts
- 1 tsp cinnamon
- Salt, to taste.

Instructions:

1. Make the bulgar wheat according to directions. Prepare other ingredients as the bulgur wheat cooks.

2. Share the cooked bulgur wheat in two bowls. Top it up with fruit, nuts, and cinnamon.

Nutritional Facts (Per Serving): Calories: 414 | Fat: 12g | Carbs: 69g | Fiber: 16g | Protein: 6g

Turkish Breakfast Wrap with Sausage, Eggs and Vegetables

Prep: 10 minutes | Cook: 15 minutes | Serves 2

Ingredients:

- 4 large eggs
- Sucuk (Turkish Sausage), sliced
- 1 medium onion, thinly sliced
- 1 medium tomato, diced
- 1 small red bell pepper, thinly sliced
- 1 small green bell pepper, thinly sliced
- ½ tsp paprika
- Salt and pepper to taste
- 4 small flatbreads (tortilla)
- Fresh parsley or cilantro
- Olive Oil for cooking

Instructions:

1. Whisk the eggs in a bowl with salt and pepper. Set this aside.
2. Drizzle some olive oil on a skillet and add in the sucuk. Cook it for 2-3 minutes. Take the crispy sucuk off the skillet.
3. Using the same skillet, add some more olive oil. Sauté the green and red bell pepper and sliced onions until they're softened, about 3-4 minutes.
4. Add the diced tomato and paprika to the sautéed vegetables. Cook for an additional 2 minutes until the tomatoes soften.
5. Add in the eggs and scramble with the vegetables.
6. Season with salt and pepper.
7. Return the cooked sucuk to the skillet and stir with the eggs.
8. Warm the flatbread in a dry skillet for a minute on each side.
9. Place some eggs and vegetable mixture on each flatbread. Sprinkle with some chopped parsley or cilantro.
10. Roll up the flatbreads to create a wrap.

Nutritional Facts (Per Serving): Calories: 385 | Fat: 21g | Carbs: 29g | Fiber: 3g | Protein: 18g

Mediterranean Breakfast Pita

Prep: 10 minutes | Cook: 5 minutes | Serves 1

Ingredients:

- Non-stick olive oil spray
- 2 eggs or 4 egg whites
- Salt and pepper to taste
- 1 cup fresh spinach – roughly chopped
- Feta
- 1 whole-wheat pita

Instructions:

1. Combine eggs or eggs whites in a small bowl and salt and pepper.
2. Spray a small non-stick skillet with olive oil cooking spray and heat over medium heat.
3. Pour in egg mixture. As eggs begin to set, gently move the spatula across the bottom and side of the skillet to form large, soft curds. Cook until eggs are thickened but not dry.
4. Add the spinach and combine until the spinach is slightly wilted.
5. Top with a sprinkle of feta and set aside.
6. Place the pita in the microwave and heat for 15 seconds. Cut in half. Fill each pocket with the egg mixture.

Nutritional Facts (Per Serving): Calories: 280 | Fat: 12g | Carbs: 24g | Fiber: 4g | Protein: 17g

Cauliflower Tabbouleh

Prep: 20 minutes | Cook: 2 minutes | Serves 4

Ingredients:

- Raw cauliflower florets
- 1 packed curly parsley, roughly chopped
- 1 cup mixed-color cherry tomatoes, halved
- 2 Persian cucumbers, sliced
- 3 Tbsp. fresh lemon juice
- ½ small red onion, finely chopped
- ½ tsp. ground cumin

- ½ tsp. kosher salt
- ½ tsp. pepper

Instructions:

1. Place the cauliflower florets in a food processor and pulse until you have finely chopped "grains". Transfer into a bowl.
2. Still in the processor bowl, add the parsley and pulse until it is very finely chopped.
3. Add the parsley into the cauliflower bowl, along with the cucumbers, red onion, cherry tomatoes, lemon juice, kosher salt, ground cumin, and pepper.
4. Mix and adjust the seasonings to your desire.

Nutritional Facts (Per Servings): Calories: 47 | Fat: 0.5g | Carbs: 10g | Fiber: 3g | Protein: 3g

Busy Morning Egg Muffins

Prep: 10 minutes | Cook: 20 minutes | Serves 12

Ingredients:

- Olive oil spray
- 1/2 cup chopped bell pepper
- 1/2 cup chopped onion
- 1/2 cup chopped zucchini
- ½ cup cheddar
- sprinkle of basil
- kosher salt and black pepper to taste
- whole eggs
- egg whites
- ½ cup milk

Instructions:

1. Preheat the oven to 350°F and coat a 12-cup muffin pan with oil spray.
2. Whisk together eggs, egg whites, and milk in a large bowl. Add your mix-ins of choice and mix thoroughly.
3. Distribute the mixture evenly into each of the 12 muffin cups. Bake for 22-24 minutes until eggs are set, checking after 15 minutes.

Nutritional Facts (Per Serving): Calories: 260 | Fat: 17g | Carbs: 7g | Fiber: 1.5g | Proteins: 23g

Lemon-Dill Asparagus

Prep: 10 minutes | Cook: 10 minutes | Serves 4

Ingredients:

- 1 bunch of fresh asparagus
- 1 lemon, zested and juiced
- 2 tbsp extra-virgin olive oil
- 1 tsp dried dill
- Salt and black pepper, to taste
- Optional: chopped fresh parsley, crumbled feta cheese

Instructions:

1. Preheat your air fryer to 190°C.
2. Trim the ends of the asparagus and wash them thoroughly.
3. Combine the Extra-virgin olive oil, lemon juice, lemon zest, dried dill, salt, and black pepper in a bowl. Mix well to create the lemon-dill seasoning.
4. Toss the trimmed asparagus in the lemon-dill seasoning, ensuring they are coated evenly.
5. Place the asparagus in the air fryer, arranging them in a single layer.
6. Air-fry for up to 10 minutes until they're tender and slightly crispy.
7. Take them out of the air fryer and serve with the chopped parsley and feta cheese.

Nutritional Facts (Per Serving): Calories: 50 | Fat: 4g | Carbs: 4g | Fiber: 2g | Protein: 2g

Tomato Toasts with Mint Yogurt and Sumac Vinaigrette

Prep: 10 minutes | Cook: 0 minutes | Serves 4

Ingredients:

- ½ cup plain Greek yogurt
- ¼ cup mint, chopped
- 1 scallion, finely chopped
- 2 tsp. grated lemon zest
- 1 tsp. lemon juice
- 2 tbsp. olive oil
- ¼ tsp. cumin seed
- ¼ tsp. kosher salt
- ¼ tsp. coarsely cracked pepper
- 4 slices toasted bread
- 3 medium heirloom tomatoes, sliced

Instructions:

1. Combine the Greek yogurt, scallion, mint, and lemon zest in a bowl.
2. In a second bowl, whisk the olive oil, cumin seed, lemon juice, ground sumac, coarsely cracked pepper, and kosher salt.
3. Spread yogurt on toast, top with heirloom tomatoes, and spoon vinaigrette. Sprinkle with additional chopped scallion as you desire.

Nutrition Facts (Per Serving): Calories: 182 | Fats: 10g | Carbs: 17g | Fiber: 4g | Protein: 8g

Fried Eggs with Smoked Salmon and Lemon Cream

Prep: 10 minutes | Cook: 10 minutes | Serves: 2

Ingredients:

- 50g Smoked salmon
- 4 Eggs
- 1 tbsp Butter
- 2 tbsp Sour cream
- 3/4 tsp Lemon juice
- 1/4 tbsp Lemon peel
- 1 Chives, stalk
- 1/4 tsp Cumin leaves

Instructions:

1. In a small bowl, mix the sour cream, lemon juice, zest, and chopped cumin leaves. Mix well.
2. In another bowl, lightly beat the eggs, salt, and pepper.
3. Melt the butter in a frying pan over medium heat.
4. Add chopped spring onions and pass for 1 minute. Then pour the eggs and cook, stirring constantly, for 1 minute. Arrange on two plates.
5. Top with thinly sliced fish and sprinkle with lemon cream.

Nutritional Facts (per serving): Calories: 192 | Fat: 15.3 g. | Protein: 11.7 g. | Carbs: 1.2 g

MEDITERRANEAN LUNCH RECIPES

Mussels with Cheese

Prep: 3 minutes | Cook: 20 minutes | Serves: 4

Ingredients:

- 450g Mussels
- 150ml White dry wine
- 225g Cheese
- 225g Cream
- 1/2 Onions head
- 2 tbsp Olive oil
- 1 tbsp Parsley, chopped
- 2 Garlic, cloves

Instructions:

1. Chop up the onions and garlic lightly browned in olive oil. Pour in the thawed mussels in this mixture, keep them a little on the fire, and add the wine.
2. Wait until the alcohol is half evaporated. Add the cheese, parsley, and black pepper.
3. When the cheese melts in the wine, add cream to the eye, boil it, and remove it from the heat.

Nutritional info (Per Serving): Calories: 115 | Fat: 7.7g. | Protein: 6.2 g. | Carbs: 2g |

Meal-Prep Falafel Bowls with Tahini Sauce

Prep: 4 minutes | Cook: 20 minutes | Serves 4

Ingredients:

- 225g package of frozen prepared falafel
- ⅔ cup water
- ½ cup whole-wheat couscous
- 450g bag steam-in-bag fresh green beans
- 1/2 cup Tahini Sauce
- ¼ cup pitted Kalamata olives
- ¼ cup crumbled feta cheese

Instructions:

1. Prepare the falafel according to package directions and set aside to cool.
2. Boil some water in a small saucepan. Pour in and stir the couscous, cover, and remove from heat. Allow to stand until the liquid is absorbed, about 5 minutes. Fluff with a fork; set aside.
3. Refrigerate the tahini sauce.
4. Place the green beans first, then top up with couscous, falafel, olives, and feta. Seal and refrigerate for up to 4 days.
5. Dress with tahini sauce just before eating.

Nutrition Facts (Per Serving): Calories: 500 | Fat: 27g | Carbs: 55g | Fiber: 11g | Protein: 15g

Chinese Cabbage with Mint and Green Peas

Prep: 4 minutes | Cook: 5 minutes | Serves: 4

Ingredients

- 110g Green pea
- 1/2 Chinese cabbage
- 1 Chili pepper
- 2 tbsp Sesame oil
- 1 Fresh min bundle
- 1 tbsp Rice vinegar
- 1 tbsp Soy sauce

Instructions:

1. Heat the wok, pour the sesame oil, and then the soy sauce with vinegar.
2. Add chopped green peas, fry for 30 seconds, then add noodles of chopped cabbage and fry for one more minute.
3. Add the mint and chopped chili peppers and mix. Turn off the heat and cover with a lid. Let it brew for a couple of minutes and serve.

Nutritional info (Per serving): Calories: 77 | Fat: 5.7g | | Carbs: 5.9g | Fiber: 2.2g | Protein: 2g

Crispy Smoked Tofu & Coleslaw Wraps

Prep: 7 minutes | Cook: 13 minutes | Serves 4

Ingredients:

- 3 tbsp mayonnaise
- 3 tbsp grapeseed or canola oil
- 1 ½ tbsp lemon juice
- ⅛ tsp salt
- ¼ tsp ground pepper
- 4 cups coleslaw mix
- 1 medium scallion, sliced
- 220g package smoked tofu, cut into ½-inch pieces (see Tip)
- 1 tbsp cornstarch
- 4 medium whole-wheat wraps

Instructions:

1. Whisk mayonnaise, 1 tbsp oil, lemon juice, salt, and pepper in a medium bowl. Add coleslaw mix and scallion and toss to coat.
2. Toss tofu with cornstarch in a medium bowl. Heat the remaining 2 tbsp oil in a medium nonstick skillet over medium-high heat.
3. Add the tofu and cook, stirring occasionally, until crispy and browned, about 5 minutes.
4. Serve the tofu and slaw in wraps, with lemon wedges, if desired.

Nutrition Facts (Per Serving): Calories: 488 | Fat: 22g | Carbs: 46g | Fiber: 4g | Protein: 15g

Scallop Ceviche

Prep: 5 minutes | Cook: 5 minutes | Serves: 4

Ingredients:

- 2 Lime
- 190g Scallop
- 25g Ginger
- 25g Cilantro
- 25ml Olive oil
- 1 tbsp Soy sauce
- 2 Garlic, clove
- Pepper black ground, to taste

Instructions:

1. Mix the juice of two lemons with a fork in any suitable container with lightly salted soy sauce.
2. Add chopped hard garlic cloves. Add the black pepper, coarse sea salt, grated ginger, grape seed oil, and coarsely chopped fresh cilantro leaves. Stir.

3. Cut the scallop mussels into thin slices, cover with sauce, and roast for five minutes.

Nutritional info (Per Serving): Calories: 89 | Fat: 4.5g | Protein: 7.1g | Carbs: 5.8g | Protein: 7.1g

Salmon Rice Bowl

Prep: 10 minutes | Cook: 15 minutes | Serves 2

Ingredients:

- 113g salmon, preferably wild
- 1 tsp avocado oil
- ⅛ tsp kosher salt
- 1 cup instant brown rice
- 1 cup water
- 2 tbsp mayonnaise
- 1 ½ tsp Sriracha
- 1 ½ tsp 50%-less-sodium tamari
- 1 tsp mirin
- ½ tsp freshly grated ginger
- ¼ tsp crushed red pepper
- ⅛ tsp kosher salt
- ½ ripe avocado, chopped
- ½ cup chopped cucumber
- ¼ cup spicy kimchi
- 12 (4 inch) sheets nori (roasted seaweed)

Instructions:

1. Set the oven temperature to 200ºC. Put foil on a small baking sheet with a rim. Place the salmon on the pan, season with salt, and drizzle with oil. Bake for 8 to 10 minutes.
2. Put the rice and water in a small saucepan and cook it as directed on the package.
3. In a small bowl, combine Sriracha and mayonnaise; leave aside.
4. In a separate small bowl, whisk together the tamari, ginger, mirin, crushed red pepper, and salt; put aside.
5. Separate the rice into two bowls. Add kimchi, cucumber, avocado, and salmon on top. Drizzle with the mayonnaise and tamari mixtures. If desired, mix the dishes and serve with nori.

Nutrition Facts (Per Serving): Calories: 481 | Fat: 25g | Carbs: 47g | Fiber: 6g | Protein: 18g

Chicken with Tomatoes, Prunes, Cinnamon, and Wine

Prep: 5 minutes | Cook: 30 minutes | Serves: 6

Ingredients:

- 1 Chicken
- 225g Tomatoes
- 266g Dry white wine
- 16 Prunes without stones
- 145ml Water
- 2½ tbsp Butter
- 2 tbsp red wine vinegar
- 2 tsp Sugar
- 1 Cinnamon stick

Instructions:

1. Cut the chicken into eight parts, and season with salt and pepper to taste. Fry the pieces in butter in a heavy skillet for 5 minutes.
2. After roasting, put all the chicken pieces tightly in the pan, add the wine, and bring to a boil for 4 minutes.
3. Add water to the pan, peeled and chopped tomatoes, one cinnamon stick, salt, pepper, and boil again.
4. Continue to cook, covered with a lid, on low heat for 20 minutes.
5. Add the chopped prunes, vinegar, and sugar, and boil again. After turning down the heat, cover and cook for 10 minutes. Remove the chicken pieces from the pan, put on a dish and cover with foil.
6. Bring the sauce remaining in the pan to a boil and cook on high heat for 8-10 minutes. The sauce should thicken.
7. Serve with cooked tomato and prune sauce.

Nutritional info per serving: Calories: 160 | Fat: 9.5 g | Protein: 11.3 g | Carbs: 5.8 g

Organic Mini Minty Lamb Koftas

Prep: 5 minutes | Cook: 10 minutes | Serves 4

Ingredients:

- 250g organic lean minced lamb
- 1 large organic carrot, grated
- 2 organic spring onions, finely sliced
- ½ clove of organic garlic, crushed
- 50g fresh organic breadcrumbs
- 2 tsp organic tomato paste
- ½ dessert spoon fresh organic mint, roughly chopped
- ½ dessert spoon fresh organic coriander, roughly chopped

Instructions:

1. Assemble all the ingredients in a large bowl.
2. Mix with a wooden spoon. Cover with cling film and place in the fridge for 30 minutes.
3. When the mix is cool and you are ready to cook, shape the mix into small kofta-shaped pieces.
4. To cook, place the kofta under the grill for 10–15 minutes until cooked through and golden in color.
5. Serve with Yogurt, some pieces of warmed naan, and a few wedges of cucumber.

Nutritional Facts (Per Serving): Calories: 212 | Fat: 12.8g | Carbs: 7.9g | Fiber: 1.5g | Protein: 17.5g

Chicken Fajita Soup

Prep: 3 minutes | Cook: 35 minutes | Serves 6

Ingredients:

- 1 tbsp extra-virgin olive oil
- 1 cup chopped yellow onion
- 1 cup chopped red bell pepper
- 1 cup chopped yellow bell pepper
- 1½ tbsp minced garlic
- 2½ tsp chili powder
- 1½ tsp ground cumin
- 1 tsp smoked paprika
- ½ tsp dried oregano
- ½ tsp salt
- 4 cups reduced-sodium chicken broth
- 820g fire-roasted diced tomatoes, undrained
- 425g no-salt-added black beans, rinsed
- ⅓ cup chopped fresh cilantro
- 2 tbsp lime juice
- 2 cups shredded rotisserie chicken
- 3 tbsp reduced-fat sour cream
- 6 tbsp tricolor tortilla strips
- 1 avocado, sliced

Instructions:

1. Heat a tbsp oil in a large pot over medium heat. Add the onion, red and yellow bell pepper, and cook, stirring occasionally, for about 5 minutes.
2. Add garlic, chili powder, cumin, paprika, oregano, and salt; continue cooking, stirring constantly, for 1 to 2 minutes.
3. Stir in broth, black beans, cilantro, undrained tomatoes, and lime juice; reduce heat to medium-low and let it simmer, uncovered and stirring occasionally, until the flavors meld, about 20 minutes.
4. Add the shredded chicken; simmer, undisturbed, for 5 minutes.

5. Serve with sour cream, 6 tbsp tortilla strips, and avocado slices in the bowls before serving.

Nutrition Facts (Per Serving): Calories: 312 | Fat: 11g | Carbs: 31g | Fiber: 10g | Protein: 25g

Grenadian Cod and Orange Salad with Olives

Prep: 4 minutes | Cook: 30 minutes | Serves 4

Ingredients:

- 450g potatoes, whole
- Ground Espelette pepper, to taste
- Salt
- 225g fresh cod fillet, centre-cut, skinless
- 3 large or four medium tart, sweet oranges
- 1 medium white onion, finely chopped
- 2 small tomatoes, blanched, peeled
- 1 pomegranate
- 4 tbsp black olives, chopped (a bitter, oily, wrinkled variety)
- 115ml extra-virgin olive oil
- 1-2 tbsp white wine vinegar

Instructions:

1. Boil the clean potatoes without peeling off the skin. Take it from the heat after 15-20 minutes.
2. Peel and cut into small dice.
3. Lightly salt and sear the cod on both sides in a hot pan until you get a nice toasted brown crust. Just cooked through, then set aside.
4. Peel the oranges, divide them into 16 segments, and roughly chop the rest into chunky pieces.
5. Finely chop the onion.
6. In a bowl, combine the diced potatoes, chopped onion, flaked cod, chopped orange pieces, and tomato. Dress these ingredients with chopped olives, olive oil, white wine vinegar, Espelette pepper, and salt to taste.
7. Fold together the ingredients to incorporate all the flavors well and chill for at least an hour.
8. Serve with pomegranate seeds and serve chilled.

Nutritional Facts (Per Serving): Calories: 334 | Fat: 19.8g | Carbs: 28.9g | Fiber: 4.8g | Protein: 17.5g

Baked Prawns with Tomatoes and Feta

Prep: 10 minutes | Cook: 15 minutes | Serves 2

Ingredients:

- 1 tbsp olive oil
- 1 medium onion, diced
- 2 cloves garlic, crushed
- 2 (400g) cans of no-salt-added diced tomatoes, with their juices
- 4 tbsp finely-chopped fresh flat-leaf parsley
- 1 tbsp finely-chopped fresh dill
- 575g medium prawns, peeled and deveined
- 1/4 tsp salt
- 1/4 tsp freshly-ground black pepper
- 150g (approx) crumbled feta cheese

Instructions:

1. Preheat the oven to 220°C.
2. Heat the oil in an oven-proof skillet over a medium-high heat. Add the onion and cook, stirring, until softened about three minutes, then add the garlic and cook for one minute.
3. Add the tomatoes and bring to a boil. Reduce the heat to medium-low and let simmer for five minutes until the tomato juices thicken.
4. Remove from the heat. Stir in the parsley, dill, and shrimp, and season with salt and pepper. Sprinkle the feta over the top. Bake for 12 minutes.

Nutritional Facts (Per Serving): Calories: 283 | Fat: 13.9g | Carbs: 10.4g | Fiber: 2.3g | Protein: 33.2g

Ben Tish's Duck and Fig Ponchos

Prep: 5 minutes | Cook: 15 minutes | Serves: 4

Ingredients:

- 8x12cm skewers soaked in water
- 200g duck breast, skin on and diced into 3cm cubes
- 2 fresh figs cut into four slices
- 500ml orange juice
- 50ml muscatel or white wine vinegar

- Sea salt and black pepper
- Olive oil for cooking

Instructions:

1. Alternate the cubes of duck and slices of fig onto the skewers until you have three pieces of each on each skewer.
2. Pour the orange juice and vinegar into a small saucepan and keep on high heat until slightly thickened. Refrigerate in the fridge for a couple of hours.
3. Heat a grill pan to maximum heat; remove the skewers from the fridge and wipe off any excess marinade. Season with salt and pepper and lay on the grill.
4. Cook for 2 minutes until the meat is lightly charred, then turn over and repeat for 3 minutes. Turn down the heat and cook for 2 minutes until the duck is cooked pink.
5. Place the skewers in a warm spot and pour over the remaining marinade.

Nutritional Facts (Per Serving): Calories: 312 | Fat: 14.2g | Carbs: 21.5g | Fiber: 2.1g | Protein: 23.8g

Linguine with Sun-dried Tomatoes. Olives, and Lemon

Prep: 5 minutes | Cook: 12 minutes | Serves 4

Ingredients:

- 450g linguine pasta
- 1 cup chopped or julienned sun-dried tomatoes in oil, drained
- 1 cup medium green olives, pitted
- 30g fresh basil leaves
- 1 clove garlic, roughly chopped
- 1/3 cup extra-virgin olive oil
- Zest and juice of 1 large lemon
- ¾ cup grated Parmesan
- Salt and freshly ground black pepper

Instructions:

1. Bring a large pot of salted water to a boil over high heat. Add the pasta and cook until tender but firm to the bite, 8 to 10 minutes.
2. Drain and reserve about 1 cup of the pasta water. Place the pasta in a large serving bowl.
3. In a food processor, combine the sun-dried tomatoes, olives, basil, garlic, oil, lemon zest, and lemon juice. Pulse until blended but still chunky.
4. Add the Parmesan cheese to the pasta and toss well. Pour the tomato mixture on top and toss until the pasta is coated. Season with salt and pepper to taste.

Nutritional Facts (Per Serving): Calories: 680 | Fat: 31.5g | Carbs: 79.8g | Fiber: 6.3g | Protein: 20.2g

MEDITERRANEAN DINNER RECIPES

Spinach Ravioli with Artichokes & Olives

Prep: 5 minutes | Cook: 25 minutes | Serves 4

Ingredients:

- 450g frozen or refrigerated spinach-and-ricotta ravioli
- ½ cup drained sun-dried
- 2 tbsp tomato oil
- ¼ cup finely chopped shallot
- 3 cloves garlic, thinly sliced
- ¼ cup unsalted butter, cubed
- 180g frozen quartered artichoke hearts, thawed
- 255g no-salt-added cannellini beans, rinsed
- ¼ cup pitted Kalamata olives, sliced
- ¼ cup chopped fresh basil
- 3 tbsp toasted pine nuts

Instructions:

1. Boil a large pot of water and cook the ravioli according to package directions. Drain the ravioli and mix with sun-dried tomato oil.
2. Heat the remaining sun-dried tomato oil in a large nonstick skillet over medium heat. Add shallot, and stir until soft.
3. Add sliced garlic and stir for 30 seconds.
4. Add water; bring to a simmer. Stir in cubed butter, melting one piece at a time.
5. Add thawed artichokes and rinsed beans and cook for 2 to 3 minutes.
6. Fold in the cooked ravioli, sun-dried tomatoes, olives, basil, and pine nuts until well coated in the sauce and heated through, for about 1 minute.

Nutritional Facts (Per Serving): Calories: 749 | Fats: 41g | Carbs: 5g | Fiber: 9g | Protein: 25g

Feta & Roasted Red Pepper Stuffed Chicken Breast

Prep: 10 minutes | Cook: 15 minutes | Serves 4

Ingredients:

- ¼ cup crumbled feta cheese
- ¼ cup chopped roasted red bell peppers
- ¼ cup chopped fresh spinach
- 1/8 cup Kalamata olives, pitted and quartered
- 1 tbsp chopped fresh basil
- 1 tbsp chopped fresh flat-leaf parsley
- 1 cloves garlic, minced
- 4 boneless, skinless chicken breasts
- Salt to taste
- ½ tsp ground pepper
- 1 tbsp extra-virgin olive oil
- 1 tbsp lemon juice

Instructions:

1. Preheat oven to 200°C. Mix feta, roasted red peppers, spinach, olives, basil, parsley, and garlic in a medium bowl.
2. Cut a horizontal slit through each chicken breast to form a pocket. Stuff each breast pocket with the feta mixture and hold it using wooden picks. Sprinkle the chicken evenly with salt and pepper.
3. Heat oil in a large oven-safe skillet over medium-high heat. Arrange the stuffed breasts in the pan and cook until golden.
4. Carefully flip the chicken; transfer the pan to the oven. Bake for 20 to 25 minutes.
5. Drizzle the chicken evenly with lemon juice. And serve.

Nutrition Facts (Per Serving): Calories: 179 | Fat:7g | Carbs: 2g | Fiber: 0g | Protein: 24g

Walnut-Rosemary Crusted Salmon

Prep: 10 minutes | Cook: 10 minutes | Serves 4

Ingredients:

- 2 tsp Dijon mustard
- 1 clove garlic, minced
- ¼ tsp lemon zest
- 1 tsp lemon juice
- 1 tsp chopped fresh rosemary
- ½ tsp honey
- ½ tsp kosher salt
- ¼ tsp crushed red pepper
- 3 tbsp panko breadcrumbs
- 3 tbsp finely chopped walnuts
- 1 tsp extra-virgin olive oil
- 450g skinless salmon fillet, fresh or frozen
- Olive oil cooking spray
- Chopped fresh parsley and lemon wedges for garnish

Instructions:

1. Preheat oven to 210°C. Line a large-rimmed baking sheet with parchment paper.
2. Combine mustard, garlic, lemon zest, lemon juice, rosemary, honey, salt, and crushed red pepper in a small bowl. Combine panko, walnuts, and oil in another small bowl.
3. Place salmon on the prepared baking sheet. Spread the mustard mixture over the fish and sprinkle with the panko mixture. Lightly coat with cooking spray.
4. Bake for 12 minutes.
5. Sprinkle with parsley and serve with lemon wedges, if desired.

Nutritional Facts (Per Serving): Calories: 222 | Fat: 12g | Carbs: 4g | Fiber: 0.9g | Protein: 24g

Padma Lakshmi's Tandoori Chicken Salad

Prep: 5 minutes | Cook: 30 minutes | Serves 4

Ingredients:

- 1 cup non-fat plain yogurt
- 2 tsp garam masala
- 1 tsp ground ginger
- 1 tsp minced garlic
- 1 tsp ground turmeric
- 1 tsp salt
- 1 jalapeño pepper
- 680g boneless, skinless chicken breasts,
- 1 tbsp of avocado oil
- 3 cups shredded iceberg lettuce
- 3 cups shredded red cabbage
- 3 cups diced plum tomatoes
- 2 cups sliced cucumber
- 1½ cups diced jicama
- 1 cup sliced radishes
- 1 small bunch scallions, finely chopped
- 1 cup cilantro leaves, finely chopped
- Juice of 2 small lemons, or to taste

Instructions:

1. Whisk yogurt, ginger, garam masala, turmeric, garlic, salt, and jalapeño in a shallow dish. Add chicken and mix. Refrigerate while preparing the vegetables.
2. Combine cabbage, lettuce, tomatoes, cucumber, radishes, scallions, jicama, and cilantro in a large bowl; toss to combine.
3. Heat up oil in a large nonstick skillet. Cook the chicken and marinade for 6 to 8 minutes.

4. Transfer the chicken and the pan juices to the bowl with the salad. Add lemon juice to taste and mix.

Nutrition Facts (Per Serving): Calories: 245 | Fat: 6g | Carbs: 16g | Fiber: 5g | Protein: 32g

Asparagus Risotto

Prep: 3 minutes | Cook: 35 minutes | Serves 4

Ingredients:

- 540g Fresh asparagus
- 540g Chicken broth
- 140g Risotto rice
- 1 Onion
- 55g Parmesan cheese, grated
- 4 tbsp Olive oil
- 3 tbsp Cream
- Ground black pepper, to taste

Instructions:

- Wash the asparagus and cut the tops. Boil the stems in boiling water until soft.
- Drain the prepared asparagus and transfer it to a chicken broth blender. Blend, pour into a frying pan and boil.
- Cook asparagus tops in boiling water for 1 minute. Drain and cool in ice water.
- Heat the olive oil in a large frying pan, add the finely chopped onion, and lightly fry. Add rice, salt, and spices and mix well.
- Add a ladle of hot broth with asparagus, stirring constantly, then add another soup ladle, and so on. Simmer for about 20 minutes until rice is cooked.
- Add the parmesan and cream and gently stir in the boiled asparagus. Serve hot.

Nutritional info (Per Serving): Calories: 105 | Fat: 4.7g | Protein: 3.5 g. | Carbs: 12.3 g.

One-Skillet salmon with Fennel & Sun-dried Tomato Couscous

Prep: 5 minutes | Cook: 30 minutes | Serves 4

Ingredients:

- 1 lemon

- 560g salmon, skinned and cut into 4 portions
- ¼ tsp salt
- ¼ tsp ground pepper
- 4 tbsp sun-dried tomato pesto, divided
- 2 tbsp extra-virgin olive oil, divided
- 2 medium fennel bulbs, cut into 1/2-inch wedges; fronds reserved
- 1 cup Israeli couscous, preferably whole-wheat
- 3 scallions, sliced
- 1 ½ cups low-sodium chicken broth
- ¼ cup sliced green olives
- 2 tbsp toasted pine nuts
- 2 cloves garlic, sliced

Instructions:

1. Zest lemon and reserve the zest. Cut the lemon into 8 slices. Season salmon with salt and pepper and spread pesto on each piece.
2. Heat some oil in a large skillet and add half the fennel; cook until brown on the bottom. Transfer to a plate.
3. Reduce heat to medium and repeat with the remaining oil and fennel. Transfer to the plate. Add couscous and scallions to the pan; cook, stirring frequently, until the couscous is lightly toasted, 1 to 2 minutes.
4. Stir in broth, olives, pine nuts, garlic, the reserved lemon zest, and the remaining pesto.
5. Nestle the fennel and salmon into the couscous. Top the salmon with the lemon slices. Cook till the couscous is tender for 4 minutes.

Nutritional Facts (Per Serving): Calories: 543 | Fat: 24g | Carbs: 46g | Fiber: 8g | Protein: 38g

BBQ Shrimp with Garlicky Kale & Parmesan-Herb Couscous

Prep: 7 minutes | Cook: 20 minutes | Serves: 4

Ingredients:

- 1 cup low-sodium chicken broth
- ¼ tsp poultry seasoning
- ⅔ cup whole-wheat couscous
- ⅓ cup grated Parmesan cheese
- 1 tbsp butter
- 3 tbsp extra-virgin olive oil, divided
- 8 cups chopped kale
- ¼ cup water
- 1 large clove garlic, smashed
- ¼ tsp crushed red pepper
- ¼ tsp salt
- 450g peeled and deveined raw shrimp
- ¼ cup barbecue sauce

Instructions:

1. Combine broth and poultry seasoning in a medium saucepan and boil. Stir in couscous. Remove from heat, and cover. Add in Parmesan and butter.
2. Meanwhile, heat some oil in a large skillet over medium-high heat. Add kale and cook, stirring, until bright green, 1 to 2 minutes.
3. Add water, cover, and cook, stirring occasionally, until the kale is tender. Make a well in the center of the kale and add oil, garlic, and crushed red pepper;
4. Stir in the garlic oil into the kale, season with salt, and transfer to a bowl.
5. Add the remaining oil and shrimp to the pan. Cook for about 2 minutes.
6. Remove from heat and stir in barbecue sauce. Serve the shrimp with the kale and couscous.

Nutrition Facts (Per Serving): Calories: 414 | Fat: 17g | Carbs: 36g | Fiber: 5g | Protein: 32g

Seafood Ravioli in Cream Cheese Sauce

Prep: 15 minutes | Cook: 45 minutes | Serves: 6

Ingredients:

- 350g Milk
- 295g Cream
- 280g Wheat flour
- 3 Egg
- 115ml Dry white wine
- 110g Butter
- 110g Shrimps, peeled
- 110g Scallops
- 4 tbsp Parsley, chopped1
- 55g Parmesan cheese, grated
- 1 tbsp Olive oil
- 1 Egg yolk
- Garlic, clove

Instructions:

1. Sift the flour with salt into a large bowl. Beat eggs, olive oil, and water and slowly stir in the flour.
2. Knead well and place in a greased bowl. Cover with foil and leave for half an hour.
3. Mix softened butter, chopped garlic, parsley, finely chopped scallops, and finely chopped shrimp.
4. Roll out the dough very thinly, cut into small circles, greasing with yolk. Spread the stuffing on each circle and close the edges tightly.
5. Boil the ravioli in salted boiling water for about 6 minutes. Drain water.

6. Melt the remaining butter in a saucepan, add the flour, and fry over low heat for 2 minutes.
7. Remove from heat and stir in milk, cream, and wine. Return to the fire and stir until the sauce thickens. Bring to a boil and cook for 5 minutes. Add the parmesan and the remaining parsley.
8. Remove from heat, and serve in a sauceboat.

Nutritional facts (per serving): Calories: 212 | Fat: 13.8 g. | Protein: 6.8 g. | Carbs: 14.2 g

One Pot Beef Stew

Prep: 10 minutes | Cook: 30 minutes | Serves 4

Ingredients:

- 400 g Beef
- 250 g Mushrooms
- 200 g Brussels sprouts
- 1-2 pcs Bell peppers
- 1 cup Chicken/vegetable broth
- 3 cloves Garlic
- 150 ml Heavy cream
- 1 tsp Thyme
- 1 sprig Rosemary
- 1/2 tsp Chili flakes
- Pepper and Salt to taste

Instructions:

1. Cut up the meat into medium-sized cubes.
2. Heat up a frying pan. Add some olive oil and fry the beef cubes on both sides until they're slightly crispy. Then remove.
3. Slice some bell peppers and cut the mushrooms into 4-6 cubes. Add more olive oil into the pan and cook the mushrooms for a few minutes.
4. Add garlic, mix, and cook for another minute or two. Add the sliced bell peppers and cook for another few minutes.
5. Mix in the Brussels sprouts and season with salt and pepper.
6. Add rosemary, thyme, and chili flakes to the pan. Mix and add the meat. Pour in chicken or vegetable broth to cover meat and vegetables halfway.
7. Let it simmer on low heat for 20-30 minutes.
8. Pour in heavy cream, mix, and taste for seasoning. Let the cream bubble, then turn off the heat. Finally, add a handful of fresh or dried parsley.

Nutritional Facts (Per Serving): Calories: 390 | Fat: 26.2g | Carbs: 12.3g | Fiber: 3.8g | Protein: 32.5g

Linguine with Creamy White Clam Sauce

Prep: 3 minutes | Cook: 15 minutes | Serves 4

Ingredients:

- 225g whole-wheat linguine
- 450g container chopped clams
- 3 tbsp extra-virgin olive oil
- 3 cloves garlic, chopped
- ¼ tsp crushed red pepper
- 1 tbsp lemon juice
- ¼ tsp salt
- 1 large tomato, chopped
- ¼ cup chopped fresh basil,
- 2 tbsp heavy cream

Instructions:

1. Place a large saucepan of water to boil. Put in the pasta and cook until it's tender, about 8 minutes, or according to package directions. Drain.
2. As the pasta cooks, drain the clams, reserving 3/4 cup of the liquid.
3. Heat oil in a skillet over medium-high heat.
4. Add garlic and crushed red pepper and cook, stirring, for 30 seconds. Add the reserved clam liquid, lemon juice, and salt; bring to a simmer and cook until slightly reduced, for 2 to 3 minutes. Add tomato and the clams; bring to a simmer and cook for 1 minute more. Remove from heat.
5. Stir in basil and cream (or half-and-half). Add the pasta and toss to coat with the sauce. Garnish with more basil, if desired.

Nutritional Facts (Per Serving): Calories: 421 | Fat: 17g | Carbs: 52g | Fiber: 8g | Protein: 22g

Bean Counter Chowder

Prep: 5 minutes | Cook: 25 minutes | Serves 4

Ingredients:

- 1/2 cup chopped onion
- 1 tbsp canola oil
- 1 garlic clove, minced
- 1 medium tomato, chopped
- 1 can chicken or vegetable broth
- 3/4 cups water

- 1/2 tsp each dried basil, oregano, and celery flakes
- 1/4 tsp pepper
- 2 cans great Northern beans, rinsed and drained
- 1 cup uncooked elbow macaroni
- 1 tbsp minced parsley

Instructions:

1. Using a large saucepan, sauté onion in oil until tender. Add garlic; cook 1 minute longer.
2. Add tomato; simmer for 5 minutes. Add broth, water, and seasonings. Bring to a boil; cook for 5 minutes. Add beans and macaroni; return to a boil.
3. Reduce heat; simmer, uncovered, until macaroni is tender, about 15 minutes. Sprinkle with parsley.

Nutritional Facts (Per Serving): Calories: 196 | Fat: 3g | Carbs: 2g | Fiber: 9g | Protein: 10g

Chicken Adobo

Prep: 15 minutes | Cook: 20 minutes | Serves 6

Ingredients:

- 2 tbsp vegetable oil
- 1,350g chicken, cut into pieces
- 1 large onion, quartered and sliced
- 2 tbsp minced garlic
- ⅔ cup low-sodium soy sauce
- ⅓ cup white vinegar
- 1 tbsp garlic powder
- 2 tsp black pepper
- 1 bay leaf

Instructions:

1. Pour some vegetable oil into a large skillet placed over medium-high heat. Cook the chicken pieces until golden brown, 2 to 3 minutes per side. Transfer the chicken to a plate.
2. Add onion and garlic to the skillet; cook until softened and brown, for about 3 to 5 minutes.
3. Pour in soy sauce and vinegar and season with garlic powder, black pepper, and bay leaf.
4. Return chicken to pan, increase heat to high, and bring to a boil. Reduce heat to medium-low, cover, and simmer until chicken is tender and cooked through 35 to 40 minutes.

Nutritional Facts (Per Serving):

Calories:361 | Fat:22g | Carbs:7g | Fiber: 1g | Protein: 33g

Moroccan Chicken Pastilla

Prep: 15 minutes | Cook: 15 minutes | Serves 4

Ingredients:

- 8 overcooked and tender chicken pieces
- 3 bay leaves
- 1 onion, peeled
- salt and pepper
- 3-4 tbsp olive oil
- 2 onions, finely diced
- 1/2 cup chopped roasted almonds
- 1/2 bunch cilantro, finely chopped
- 2 tsp cinnamon
- 2 tbsp sugar
- 1 tsp paprika
- 1 tsp cumin
- 1 tsp sea salt
- 12 feuilles de brick, Moroccan pastry paper or filo dough,
- Olive oil for frying

Instructions:

1. Place the chicken on a cutting board to cool and shred it.
2. Heat up a large pan on medium heat. Add olive oil and sauté onions until golden. Add in the shredded chicken, almonds, cilantro, and 2-3 tbsp water. Season with cinnamon, sugar, paprika, cumin and salt. Stir well and cook over low heat until the mixture thickens about 10 minutes. Take off the fire and allow it to cool.
3. On a clean surface, cut the round brick paper in half. Place a tbsp of the chicken mixture off center and fold the bottom paper over the mixture. Tuck the right side over the mixture and keep on folding until you get a triangle, ensuring the edges are wet to "seal" the fold.
4. Heat a small saucepan, filling it with a few inches of oil on medium-high. Fry the pastilla until it's golden. Drain on a paper towel and sprinkle some powdered sugar to serve.

Nutritional Facts (Per Serving): Calories: 820 | Fat: 28.9g | Carbs: 31.2g | Fiber: 3.9g | Protein: 38.4g

One-Pan Chicken Parmesan Pasta

Prep: 10 minutes | Cook: 25 minutes | Serves 4

Ingredients:

- 2 tbsp extra-virgin olive oil
- ¼ cup whole-wheat panko breadcrumbs
- 1 tbsp plus 1 tsp minced garlic, divided
- 450g boneless, skinless chicken breast, cut into ½-inch pieces
- 1 tsp Italian seasoning
- ¼ tsp salt
- 3 cups low-sodium chicken broth
- 1½ cups crushed tomatoes
- 225g whole-wheat penne
- ½ cup shredded mozzarella cheese
- ¼ cup shredded Parmesan cheese
- ¼ cup chopped fresh basil

Instructions:

1. Heat 1 tbsp of olive oil in a large broiler-safe skillet on medium-high heat. Add the panko and 1 tsp garlic. Cook, stirring for 2 minutes, until the panko is golden brown. Transfer to a small bowl and set aside. Wipe out the pan.
2. Heat the remaining tbsp of oil in the pan on medium-high heat. Add the chicken, Italian seasoning, salt, and the garlic. Cook, stirring frequently, until the chicken is no longer pink on the outside, for about 2 minutes. Add 3 cups broth, 1 1/2 cups tomatoes, and the penne. Bring to a boil and cook, uncovered, stirring frequently, until the penne is cooked and the sauce has reduced and thickened, 15 to 20 minutes.
3. As this cooks, put an oven rack in the upper third of the oven. Preheat the broiler to high. When the pasta is cooked, sprinkle some mozzarella over the penne mixture. Place the pan under the broiler; broil until the mozzarella is bubbling and beginning to brown about 1 minute. Top up with the panko mixture, Parmesan, and basil.

Nutrition Facts (Per Serving): Calories: 538 | Fat: 17g | Carbs: 56g | Fiber: 7g | Protein: 41g

Creamy Seafood Bisque

Prep: 15 minutes | Cook: 25 minutes | Serves 4

Ingredients:

- ¼ cup butter, cubed
- 1 medium red onion, chopped
- ½ cup sliced fresh mushrooms
- 1 garlic cloves, minced
- ¼ cup all-purpose flour
- ½ tsp salt
- ½ tsp coarsely ground pepper
- 1 tbsp tomato paste
- 470ml chicken broth
- 1 cup whole baby clams, drained
- 110g uncooked medium shrimp, peeled and deveined
- 1 cup lump crabmeat, drained
- 1 cup heavy whipping cream
- ¼ cup shredded Parmesan cheese
- 1 green onion, thinly sliced

Instructions:

1. Heat some butter over medium-high heat in a Dutch oven. Add red onion and mushrooms; saute these for 4 minutes until tender. Add garlic; cook 1 minute longer.
2. Stir in the flour, salt, and pepper until blended; add tomato paste. Gradually whisk in broth and boil. Reduce heat; cover and let simmer for 5 minutes.
3. Finally, add in the shrimp and clams and allow to boil. Reduce the heat and let it simmer uncovered for 5-10 minutes or until shrimp turn pink. Stir in crab and cream; heat through (do not let it boil). Serve with cheese and green onions.

Nutritional Facts (Per Serving): Calories: 453 | Carbs: 12g | Fat: 36g | Fiber: 1g | Protein: 20g

Tomato and Pepper Poached Cod

Prep: 10 minutes | Cook: 30 minutes | Serves 4

Ingredients:

- 2 tbsp Extra-virgin olive oil
- 1 onion, thinly sliced
- 3 cloves garlic, minced

- 395g roasted piquillo or red peppers, drained and thinly sliced
- 790g crushed tomatoes
- 1 tsp smoked Spanish paprika
- 1 tsp kosher salt
- 1/4 tsp freshly ground black pepper
- 1 bay leaf
- 680g cod fillet, cut into four portions
- 1 tbsp minced flat-leaf parsley

Instructions:

1. Heat the olive oil in a large skillet. Add in the onion, cooking until softened and turning golden on the edges, about 5 minutes. Pour the garlic, also cook until fragrant, which is another 1 minute. Add the sliced piquillo peppers and cook, stirring occasionally, for 5 minutes.
2. Add the tomatoes, paprika, salt, pepper, and bay leaf. Reduce the heat to low and simmer for 15 minutes until the sauce thickens slightly.
3. Nestle the fish into the tomato sauce skin side up. Cook for 5 to 6 minutes, then flip and continue simmering until the fish is opaque and flakes easily, 5 to 6 minutes.
4. Serve the cod with the tomato and pepper sauce. Garnish with parsley.

Nutritional Facts (Per Serving): Calories: 218 | Fat: 8.3g | Carbs: 3.8g | Fiber: 0.8g | Protein: 30.9g

Tahini Chicken with Polenta

Prep: 10 minutes | Cook: 30 minutes | Serves 4

Ingredients:

- 1 tbsp olive oil
- 1 shallot chopped
- 1 clove garlic chopped
- 1 tbsp tomato paste
- 2 cups chicken (breast or thigh) Cut into bite-sized pieces.
- 1 cup crushed tomatoes
- 2 cups chicken stock
- 1/2 cup polenta (coarse cornmeal)
- 1/4 cup tahini
- 1 tbsp lemon juice
- 1/4 cup fresh parsley
- Salt and pepper, to taste

Instructions:

1. Heat the olive oil in a skillet on medium heat.
2. Pour in the garlic clove, shallot, and tomato paste. Fry the tomato paste until it turns brown.
3. Season the chicken with salt and pepper.

4. Add the chicken to the skillet and cook until it's browned on every side.
5. Add the crushed tomatoes to the chicken and cook on medium heat for about 20 minutes. Make sure the chicken cooks thoroughly.
6. As the chicken cooks, boil the chicken stock in a saucepan. Add the polenta and allow it simmer. Add more liquid if needed. The polenta should be soft and creamy.
7. Mix the tahini with lemon juice until smooth in a small bowl.
8. Add the polenta to the skillet with the chicken and drizzle on tahini sauce. Top with fresh parsley leaves.

Nutritional Facts (Per Serving): Calories: 350 | Fat: 15g | Carbs: 30g | Fiber: 3g | Protein: 25g

Spanish Grilled Sardines With Lemon, Garlic, and Paprika

Prep: 5 minutes | Cook: 30 minutes | Serves 4

Ingredients:

- 3 medium garlic cloves, finely minced (about 1 tbsp)
- ¼ cup Extra-virgin olive oil
- ¼ cup fresh juice from about 2 whole lemons
- 1 tsp smoked Spanish paprika
- 1/2 tsp freshly ground black pepper
- 450g fresh sardines, cleaned, scaled, and gutted
- Fine sea salt or Kosher salt
- 2 tbsp chopped fresh parsley
- Lemon wedges for serving

Instructions:

1. Mix up olive oil, garlic, lemon juice, paprika, and black pepper in a small bowl and whisk well to combine.
2. Arrange the sardines at the bottom of a baking dish (sallow) in a single layer and pour the marinade over the fish. Turn the fish over and ensure that they are coated evenly. Spoon some of the marinade into the cavity of each fish as well and set aside to marinate for 30 minutes.
3. Light up the grill and allow it to preheat for 5 minutes.
4. Place the marinaded sardines on the grill plate, grilling over direct heat until well-charred, for 2 to 3 minutes.
5. Flip the sardines over and grill until charred on the second side and cooked through, for another 2 minutes longer.
6. Garnish with chopped parsley and serve with lemon wedges.

Nutritional Facts (Per Serving): Calories: 356 | Fat: 21g | Carbs: !8g | Fiber: 5g | Protein: 29g

Baked Haddock with Baby Bell Peppers

Prep: 15 minutes | Cook: 15 minutes | Serves 4

Ingredients:

- 4 haddock fillets, 160g each
- Kosher salt
- Black pepper
- 8 baby bell peppers, any color, sliced into thin rounds
- 4 green onions, both white and green parts, trimmed and chopped
- 2 large garlic cloves, minced
- 1 1/2 tsp Greek oregano
- 1 tsp paprika
- 1 lemon, zest and juice
- Extra-virgin olive oil
- 1/4 cup finely chopped fresh parsley, plus more for serving
- Lemon wedges for serving

Instructions:

1. Place a rack in the oven and heat the oven up to 200°C.
2. Pat the fish dry on both sides and, season with kosher salt and black pepper, and then place it in a large mixing bowl.
3. Still into the fish, add the green onions, baby bell peppers, paprika, garlic, oregano and parsley. Add more salt and pepper, the lemon juice, lemon zest, and about 1/4 cup of Extra-virgin olive oil. Toss well to combine, making sure the fish and vegetables are well coated with the seasoning.
4. Transfer the fish and vegetables to a large baking dish. Bake in the heated oven until the fish flakes easily at the touch of a fork.
5. Garnish with more chopped parsley, and serve immediately with fresh lemon wedges.

Nutritional Facts (Per Serving): Calories: 187.9 | Fat: 2.7g | Carbs: 8.3g | Fiber: 2.9g | Protein: 33g

Red Lentil Soup Mix

Prep: 10 minutes | Cook: 15 minutes | Serves 4

Ingredients:

- ¼ cup dried minced onion
- 2 tbsp dried parsley flakes
- 2 tsp ground allspice
- 2 tsp ground cumin
- 2 tsp ground turmeric
- Salt
- 1 tsp garlic powder
- 1 tsp ground cardamom
- 1 tsp ground cinnamon
- 1 tsp pepper
- 1/2 tsp ground cloves
- 2 packages (450g each) dried red lentils
- 1 medium carrot, finely chopped
- 1 celery rib, finely chopped
- 1 tbsp olive oil
- 2 cans (410g each) vegetable broth

Instructions:

1. Combine the first 11 ingredients, which are all spices.
2. Rinse lentils and drain.
3. Using a large saucepan over medium-high heat, sauté carrot and celery in oil until tender. Add lentils, onion mixture and broth. Bring to a boil. Reduce heat; simmer, covered, until lentils are tender, 10-15 minutes.

Nutritional Facts (Per Servings): Calories: 257 | Fat: 4g | Carbs: 42g | Fiber: 7g | Protein: 14g

MEDITERRANEAN RICE AND PASTA DISHES

Mediterranean Rice Pilaf

Prep: 5 minutes | Cook: 25 minutes | Serves 8

Ingredients:

- 2 cups basmati rice
- Extra-virgin olive oil
- 1 small yellow onion, finely chopped
- 2 garlic cloves, minced
- 1 cup frozen peas
- 2 to 3 carrots, peeled and chopped
- Kosher salt
- ½ tsp coriander
- ½ tsp paprika
- ½ tsp Aleppo pepper
- ¼ tsp ground turmeric

Instructions:

1. Rinse the rice, then soak it in water for 10 minutes.
2. Heat 2 tbsp of Extra-virgin olive oil in a saucepan.
3. Mix in the garlic and onions, then sauté until softened. Add the peas, carrots, seasoning, spices, and kosher salt.
4. Cook until the carrots have softened.
5. Mix the drained rice into the pan and coat it with the spices. Pour in water and season with kosher salt.
6. Let this boil, then turn the heat down. Cover and simmer for 20 minutes until the rice has absorbed all the liquid.
7. Serve hot.

Nutritional Facts Per Serving: Calories: 282 | Fat: 7.4g | Carbs: 48.1g | Fiber: 3.4g | Protein: 6.6g

Lemon-Garlic Shrimp Pasta

Prep: 10 minutes | Cook: 20 minutes | Serves 4

Ingredients:

- 225g pasta - linguini, spaghetti

- 3 tbsp olive oil
- 5 garlic cloves, roughly chopped
- ½ tsp red pepper flakes
- ½ tsp cracked peppercorns
- Zest from 1 lemon
- 450g large shrimp, peeled and deveined
- Salt
- Handful of kale
- Squeeze of fresh lemon juice to taste
- ¼ cup Pecorino cheese
- ½ cup fresh Italian parsley

Instructions:

1. Prepare the pasta using the package directions. Drain, saving one cup of hot pasta water.
2. Heat some olive oil in a pan, add garlic, and sauté until fragrant; add the chili flakes, black pepper, and lemon zest, and sauté 1 minute.
3. Add in the shrimp and season with salt. Cook until it is almost cooked through, about 4 minutes. Add the kale and stir for one minute.
4. Add the pasta, mixing it well with the shrimp. Sprinkle in the cheese, lemon juice, and parsley.
5. Add the salted pasta water, pepper, Chilli flakes and mix thoroughly.
6. Take it off when the pasta is well seasoned and serve.

Nutritional Facts (Per Serving): Calories: 437 | Fat: 14g | Carbs: 45.4g | Fiber: 2.6g | Protein: 33.1g

Mushroom risotto

Prep: 7 minutes | Cook: 30 minutes | Serves 4

Ingredients:

- 6 cups low-sodium chicken stock
- 3 tbsp Extra-virgin olive oil
- 1 small yellow onion, diced
- 450g cremini mushrooms, sliced
- ½ tsp dried thyme)
- 1 tsp chopped fresh rosemary
- Freshly ground black pepper
- 1 tsp salt
- 5 garlic cloves, minced
- 1 ½ tsp balsamic vinegar
- 1 ½ cups arborio or carnaroli rice
- 3/4 cup shredded parmesan cheese
- Minced fresh parsley for garnish

Instructions:

1. Add the stock into a heated pan and let it warm as other ingredients are prepared.
2. Add olive oil into a bigger pan over medium-high heat. Add the diced

onion and sauté until soft. Stir in the sliced mushrooms, thyme, rosemary, freshly ground pepper to taste, and salt. Let this cook for about 8 minutes.
3. Add the garlic and balsamic vinegar and cook for an additional minute, then transfer to a plate.
4. Add 1 tbsp of olive oil into the same pan. Stir in the rice for about 30 seconds.
5. Pour ¾ cup of warm stock into the rice in intervals, stirring until the rice is creamy and al dente, this process will take about 25 minutes.
6. Take off the heat. Stir in the parmesan cheese and mushrooms into the risotto and serve.

Nutritional Facts (Per Serving): Calories: 340.8 | Fat: 10.9g | Carbs: 48.8g | Fiber: 2.3g | Protein: 13.2g

Bruschetta Chicken Pasta

Prep: 5 minutes | Cook: 25 minutes | Serves 4

Ingredients:

- 225g whole-wheat spaghettini
- 3 tbsp extra-virgin olive oil
- 450g boneless, skinless chicken breasts, cut into 1-inch pieces
- 1 tsp dried Italian seasoning
- 600g multicolored cherry tomatoes
- 3 cloves garlic, finely chopped
- 1 tsp salt
- ¼ tsp ground pepper
- ¼ cup dry white wine
- 1 tbsp plus 1 tsp balsamic glaze
- 30g grated Parmesan cheese
- ¼ cup thinly sliced fresh basil

Instructions:

1. Cook pasta as on the package, leaving out salt. Drain.
2. Heat some olive oil in a skillet. Add chicken and Italian seasoning and cook until cooked through. Transfer the chicken to a plate.
3. Lower the heat and, pour in tomatoes, garlic, salt, pepper, and cook until the tomatoes burst.
4. Add wine, increase the heat and stir, crushing the tomatoes. Add the pasta and chicken and mix gently, then take off the heat.
5. Drizzle some balsamic glaze and enjoy

Nutritional Facts (Per Serving): Calories: 499 | Fat: 17g | Carbs: 52g | Fiber: 8g | Protein: 34g

Maqbouleh

Prep: 10 minutes | Cook: 35 minutes | Serves 4

Ingredients:

- 500g chicken thigh fillets, thinly sliced
- 1/2 tsp ground allspice
- 100ml Extra-virgin olive oil
- 3 onions, thinly sliced
- 3 tsp baharat spice mix
- 1 tsp sumac
- Finely grated zest of 2 lemons
- 400g cherry tomatoes
- 2 cups basmati rice
- 3 cups Massel Chicken Style Liquid Stock
- Harissa, to serve
- 1 cup Greek yoghurt
- Juice of ½ lemon
- 1 tbsp tahini
- 2 Lebanese cucumbers, sliced into rounds

Instructions:

1. Heat some olive oil in a large saucepan. Stir in onion and salt until lightly caramelized. Place the onions in a bowl.
2. Add chicken, spices, and lemon zest to the pan and stir for 4 minutes to lightly color the chicken. Transfer chicken to the bowl with onion.
3. Add tomatoes to the same pan with some olive oil. Pour over half of the rice, then the chicken and onion mixture. Top with the remaining 1 cup of rice, chicken stock, and salt. Cover and let simmer for 30 minutes, then turn off the heat.
4. Mix yogurt, lemon, 2 tbsp cold water, and tahini in a bowl, stirring until well combined. Season with salt and pepper, then add in the cucumber.
5. Remove the lid from the rice, turn the pan upside down and serve with harissa and yogurt.

Nutritional Facts (Per Serving): Calories: 981 | Fat: 51.4g | Carbs: 89.6g | Fiber: 6.8g | Protein: 38.6g

One-Pot Tomato Basil Pasta

Prep: 5 minutes | Cook: 25 minutes | Serves 4

Ingredients:

- 225g whole-wheat rotini
- 1 cup water
- 2 cups low-sodium "no-chicken" broth or chicken broth
- 1 (450g) can no-salt-added diced tomatoes
- 2 tbsp extra-virgin olive oil
- 1½ tsp Italian seasoning
- ½ tsp onion powder
- ½ tsp garlic powder
- ½ tsp salt
- ¼ tsp crushed red pepper
- 6 cups baby kale or baby spinach
- ½ cup slivered basil
- Grated Parmesan cheese

Instructions:

1. Place the pasta, broth, water, tomatoes, oil, onion powder, Italian seasoning, garlic powder, salt, and crushed red pepper in a big pot. Cover and let it boil over high heat.
2. Uncover and reduce heat, stirring frequently, for 10 minutes. Stir in kale and basil until most of the liquid is absorbed, 5 minutes more.
3. Garnish with Parmesan.

Nutritional Facts (Per Serving): Calories: 339 | Fat: 10g | Carbs: 55g | Fiber: 8g | Protein: 11g

Turkish pilaf

Prep: 5 minutes | Cook: 25 minutes | Serves 6

- 60g butter
- 225g boneless lamb, cut in julienne strips
- 3 medium onions, chopped
- 1 cup walnut pieces
- 475g uncooked rice
- 1 large tomato, peeled, seeded & chopped
- 1 cup raisins
- 2 tsp Salt
- 1 tsp Pepper
- ½ tsp Sage
- ¼ tsp Allspice
- 4 cups water
- 1 tsp chopped parsley

Instructions:

1. Heat the butter and sauté the lamb until its sides turn brown and remove.
2. In the same butter, cook the onion until soft but not brown, then add the nuts and rice and cook for 5 minutes.
3. Add the tomato and stir.
4. Reduce heat to the lowest and cook until the rice is tender and all the liquid is absorbed.

5. Return the lamb to the rice and cook for 3 minutes.
6. Sprinkle on parsley or mint.

Nutritional Facts (Per Serving): Calories: 495 | Fat: 20g | Carbs: 65g | Fiber: 2.7g | Protein: 13.4g

Passion Fruit and Spicy Couscous

<u>Prep: 15 minutes | Cook: 15 minutes | Serves 4</u>

Ingredients:

- Salt
- Allspice
- 1 tsp. mixed spice
- 1 cup boiling water
- 2 tsp. extra-virgin olive oil
- ½ cup full-fat Greek yogurt
- ½ cup honey
- 1 cup couscous
- 1 tsp. orange zest
- 2 oranges, peeled and sliced
- 2 tbsp. passion fruit pulp
- 1/2 cup blueberries
- 1/2 cup walnuts, roasted and unsalted
- 2 tbsp. fresh mint

Instructions:

1. Mix the salt, allspice, mixed spice, honey, couscous, and boiling water in a bowl and cover for 10 minutes.
2. Using a fork, stir the mixture, then add the diced walnuts.
3. In another bowl, combine the passion fruit pulp, yogurt, and orange zest.
4. Dish the couscous, and top with blueberries and mint leaves.

Nutritional Facts (Per Serving): Calories: 100 | Fat: 11g | Carbs: | Fiber: | Protein: 2g

Cauliflower Rice Paella

<u>Prep: 10 minutes | Cook: 25 minutes | Serves 4</u>

Ingredients:

- 1 large head cauliflower
- 2 tbsp olive oil or avocado oil
- 1 med yellow onion, diced
- 3 cloves garlic, minced
- 1 red bell pepper, diced
- 1 cup Roma tomato, diced
- 1 tsp smoked paprika

- 1 tsp saffron threads
- Salt
- 225g chorizo sausage
- 340g raw shrimp, peeled and deveined
- ½ cup white wine
- 4 tbsp lemon juice, divided
- 1 tbsp tomato paste
- 3 tbsp fresh parsley, chopped

Instructions:

1. Pulse the cauliflower florets in a blender for 20 seconds until it resembles a rice texture. Set aside.
2. Sauté garlic and onion in a heated pan with olive oil for 3 minutes.
3. Add in the raw chorizo, and cook for 5 minutes.
4. Mix in bell pepper and cauliflower rice. Continue to sauté for 5-6 minutes.
5. Pour in tomatoes, paprika, saffron, salt, shrimp and chorizo.
6. Mix in white wine, lemon juice, and tomato paste then bring to a quick boil. Reduce the heat and simmer, for another 8-10 minutes.
7. Finally, add the remaining lemon juice and parsley for garnish. Serve warm.

Nutritional Facts (Per Serving): Calories: 400 | Fat: 20g | Carbs: 35g | Fiber: 5g | Protein: 35g

Farfalle with Tuna, Lemon, and Fennel

Prep: 5 minutes | Cook: 25 minutes | Serves 4

Ingredients:

- 170g dried whole-grain farfalle pasta
- 1 (140g) can solid white tuna
- Olive oil
- 1 cup fennel, thinly sliced
- 2 cloves garlic, minced
- ½ tsp crushed red pepper
- ¼ tsp salt
- 2 (410g) cans no-salt-added diced tomatoes, undrained
- 2 tbsp snipped fresh Italian parsley
- 1 tsp lemon peel, finely shredded

Instructions:

1. Cook pasta as dictated on package directions, minus salt; drain after.
2. Drain tuna, reserving oil. Flake tuna; set aside.
3. Add the fennel, garlic, crushed red pepper, and salt unto a heated pan

with the reserved tuna oil; stir until garlic is golden.
4. Stir in tomatoes and boil; then reduce the heat. Simmer uncovered until the mixture thickens. Stir in tuna and let this sit for 1 minute more.
5. Fold tuna mixture into pasta, stirring to combine.
6. Serve.

Nutritional Facts (Per Serving): Calories: 356 | Fat: 14g | Carbs: 43g | Fiber: 9g | Protein: 17g

Spanakorizo

Prep: 10 minutes | Cook: 20 minutes | Serves 2

Ingredients:

- 450 g fresh spinach rinsed
- Juice of half lemon
- 1 onion chopped
- Olive oil
- I tsp dry mint (preferably spearmint)
- 2 tbsp chopped dill
- 2/3 cups water
- 1/3 cup medium-grain rice
- Salt/Pepper
- 1 tbsp tomato paste

Instructions:

1. Wilt the spinach, some lemon juice, and 1 tsp olive oil, all inside a large pot. Set aside to drain.
2. Let the spinach, dry mint, and dill boil in warm water.
3. Sauté the onion using the rest of the olive oil until soft.
4. Add the rice, salt and pepper to taste and let it simmer covered for 20 minutes until the rice softens. Add warm water as needed.
5. Serve warm with a squeeze of lemon juice and a bit of feta.

Nutritional Facts (Per Serving): Calories: 350 | Fat: 12g | Carbs: 34g | Fiber: 7g | Protein: 7g

Seared Salmon with Pesto Fettuccine

Prep: 3 minutes | Cook: 20 minutes | Serves 4

Ingredients:

- 225g whole-wheat fettuccine
- ⅔ cup pesto
- 565g wild salmon, skinned and cut into 4 portions
- ¼ tsp salt
- ¼ tsp ground pepper
- Extra-virgin olive oil

Instructions:

1. In a skillet, heat olive oil whilst seasoning salmon with salt and pepper in a bowl.
2. Fry the salmon, turning once, until just opaque in the middle, 2 to 4 minutes per side.
3. Boil some water, add the fettuccine, and cook until tender. Drain and transfer to a large bowl. Toss with pesto.
4. Serve the salmon with the pasta.

Nutritional Facts (Per Serving): Calories: 603 | Fat: 28g | Carbs: 45g | Fiber: 8g | Protein: 44g

Risotto Carbonara

Prep: 10 minutes | Cook: 30 minutes | Serves 4

Ingredients:

- ¼ cup Extra-virgin olive oil
- 1 onion, finely chopped
- 1 garlic clove, finely chopped
- 200g smoky bacon, finely chopped
- 2 eggs, plus 3 yolks
- 2 cups finely grated parmesan, plus extra to serve
- 250g arborio rice
- 5 cups (1.25L) Massel Chicken Style Liquid Stock

Instructions:

1. Heat some oil in a pan. Pour in the onion, garlic, and bacon and cook until the bacon is fragrant.
2. Whisk the eggs, yolks, ground black pepper, and parmesan in a bowl.
3. Stir rice into onion mixture to coat the grains, then add stock, 1 ladleful at a time, stirring at each addition, for 20 minutes or until all the stock has been used and rice is al dente.
4. Remove from heat, cool for 2 minutes, and add the egg mixture. Stir for 2 minutes to create a rich, creamy risotto. Leave on low heat for 1 minute, then remove and season to taste.
5. Scatter extra parmesan over the rice and black pepper to serve.

Nutritional Facts (Per Serving): Calories: 620 | Fat: 38g | Carbs: 45g | Fiber: 1.5g | Protein: 25g

Spaghetti Al Pomodoro Crudo

Prep: 10 minutes | Cook: 15 minutes | Serves 6

Ingredients:

- 1 (565 g) summer-ripe tomatoes, diced
- 1/2 cup extra-virgin olive oil
- 3 medium cloves garlic, finely minced
- 25 fresh basil leaves
- Kosher salt
- 450 g dried spaghetti

Instructions:

1. Stir the tomatoes, olive oil, salt, garlic, and basil in a mixing bowl. Let this stand for at least 15 minutes.
2. In a pot of salted boiling water, cook spaghetti until al dente.
3. Transfer pasta into tomato mixture, reserving pasta cooking water.
4. Stir well to coat the pasta with tomato mixture. Add reserved pasta cooking water in bits for a saucier consistency. Season with salt and serve.

Nutritional Facts (Per Serving): Calories: 461 | Fat: 20g | Carbs: 61g | Fiber: 4g | Protein: 11g

Risi e Bisi (Venetian-style rice and peas)

Prep: 4 minutes | Cook: 30 minutes | Serves 4

Ingredients:

- 30g unsalted butter
- 2 tbsp Extra-virgin olive oil
- 1 onion, finely chopped
- 3 garlic cloves, finely chopped
- 100g pancetta or smoky bacon, finely chopped
- 1/2 cup white wine
- 295g arborio rice
- 1.5L chicken stock
- 1¼ cups finely grated parmesan
- 2 tbsp chopped mint leaves, plus whole leaves to serve
- 3 cups frozen peas
- ½ cup mascarpone
- Finely grated lemon zest to serve

Instructions:

1. Melt butter and oil in a deep frypan. Mix in the onion, garlic, and pancetta, and cook for 8-10 minutes.

2. Add wine, reduce heat, and bring to a simmer for 1 minute. Add rice, stirring to coat the grains, then add 1.25L of the stock, increase heat, and bring to a boil.
3. Reduce heat again to low. Stir every 5 minutes to release the starch from the rice.
4. After 20 minutes, season with salt and pepper, then stir in parmesan, chopped mint, peas, and the remaining 250ml stock. Cook for 1 minute to melt cheese and cook peas.
5. Take off the heat, stirring through the mascarpone. Scatter with extra parmesan, whole mint leaves, and lemon zest to serve.

Nutritional Facts (Per Serving): Calories: 615 | Fat: 32g | Carbs: 55g | Fiber: 4.5g | Protein: 21g

Pasta with Arugula and Walnut Pesto

Prep: 5 minutes | Cook: 20 minutes | Serves 4

Ingredients:

- 1 (450g) Spaghetti
- 140g Pecorino Romano cheese
- 1/2 cup Walnuts
- 1 Arugula, bundle
- 4 tbsp Olive oil
- Basil leaves, to taste
- Pepper black ground, to taste

Instructions:

1. Mix and blend olive oil, arugula, grated or sliced pecorino, and halved walnuts in a blender. Ensure the ingredients remain distinguishable in the pesto.
2. When the blended mixture is thick, like sour cream, the pesto is ready.
3. Boil the spaghetti in lightly salted water until al dente.
4. Drain and mix the pasta with freshly prepared pesto in a saucepan.
5. Put the mixture on the plates and decorate with a leaf of green basil.
6. Serve with freshly grated pecorino.

Nutritional Facts (Per Serving): Calories: 410 | Fat: 23g | Carbs: 39g | Fiber: 5g | Protein: 21g

Garlic & Seafood Couscous

Prep: 10 minutes | Cook: 20 minutes | Serves 8

Ingredients:

- 8 Scallions, Sliced
- 4 Boxes Garlic Flavored Couscous, Boiled & Drained
- 545g shrimp, Raw, Peeled, Deveined & Chopped
- 1 Cup parsley, Fresh & Chopped
- 4 Tbsp Olive Oil
- 1kg Codfish, Chopped into 1 Inch Pieces
- 1 Cup Chives, Fresh & Chopped
- Hot Sauce to Taste
- 540g. Bay Scallops
- Sea Salt & Black Pepper to Taste

Instructions:

1. Pour the scallions, codfish, shrimp, scallops, parsley, and chives in a bowl.
2. Season using salt and pepper, then heat some oil in a skillet. Mix in the seafood mixture once the oil is hot. Sauté until it turns golden, and then throw in the hot sauce. Lower the heat, and cover with a lid for it to simmer.
3. Cool for five minutes, and then divide your couscous between bowls. Top with the seafood mixture and serve warm.

Nutritional Facts (Per Serving): Calories: 548 | Fat: 14g | Carbs: 32g | Fiber: 3g | Protein: 70g

Mediterranean-Style Chicken and Rice

Prep: 5 minutes | Cook: 10 minutes | Serves 4

Ingredients:

- 2 cups White Rice
- 1 tbsp olive oil
- 4 boneless, skinless chicken breasts
- 1 can (410g) Italian-style diced tomatoes, undrained
- 1 cup frozen cut green beans
- ½ tsp salt
- ¼ tsp black pepper

Instructions:

1. Boil the rice, adding salt to taste.
2. Heat some oil in a large skillet on medium-high heat. Add chicken and cook for 4 minutes per side.
3. Add tomatoes with their liquid and green beans to the skillet. Bring to a boil. Cover and reduce heat.
4. Simmer for 5 minutes, until chicken is cooked through (75°C) and beans are crisp-tender. Stir in salt and pepper. Serve over cooked rice.

Nutritional Facts (Per Serving): Calories: 370 | Fat: 6g | Carbs: 43g | Fiber: 2.5g | Protein: 32g

Feta and Tomato Rice

Prep: 10 minutes | Cook: 5 minutes | Serves 2

Ingredients:

- 2 cups Basmati Rice
- 1/2 cup grape tomatoes, halved
- 1/4 cup feta cheese, crumbled
- 2 tbsp olive oil
- 4 fresh basil leaves, torn
- 1 tsp minced garlic
- Salt and pepper

Instructions:

1. Boil the basmati rice.
2. Toss the tomatoes, oil, feta, basil, garlic, salt and pepper.
3. Combine rice with tomato mixture.
4. Garnish with shredded, cooked chicken, chopped cured chorizo sausage, or canned beans or lentils, and enjoy.

Nutritional Facts (Per Servings): Calories: 300 | Fat: 7g | Carbs: 48g | Fiber: 1.5g | Protein: 5g

Tomato and Cherry Linguine

Prep: 10 minutes | Cook: 15 minutes | Serves 4

Ingredients:

- 905g cherry tomatoes
- 3 tbsp Extra-virgin olive oil
- 2 tbsp balsamic vinegar
- 2 tsp garlic, minced
- Pinch of fresh ground black pepper
- 337g whole-wheat linguine pasta
- 1 tbsp fresh oregano, chopped
- ¼ cup feta cheese, crumbled

Instructions:

1. Preheat your oven to 175°C.
2. Taking a large bowl, add cherry tomatoes, 2 tbsp olive oil, balsamic vinegar, garlic, pepper, and toss.
3. Spread tomatoes evenly on a lined baking sheet and roast for 15 minutes.
4. As the tomatoes roast, cook the pasta and drain.
5. Toss pasta with 1 tbsp olive oil and roasted tomatoes.

6. Serve with a topping of oregano and feta cheese.

Nutritional Facts (Per Serving): Calories: 397 | Fat: 4g | Carbs: 55g | Fiber: 3g | Protein: 13g

MEDITERRANEAN SNACKS RECIPES

Spicy Rosemary Olives

Prep: 5 minutes | Cook: 5 minutes | Serves 4

Ingredients:

- 2 cups high-quality green and black olives
- ¼ cup Extra-virgin olive oil
- 1 tsp red pepper flakes
- 2 tbsp. Fresh chopped rosemary

Instructions:

1. Heat some oil in an iron skillet
2. Mix in all ingredients.
3. Cook the mixture for 7 minutes
4. Remove from pan and store refrigerated, in a glass jar.
5. Enjoy served chilled.

Nutritional Facts (Per Serving): Calories: 114 | Fat: 12g | Carbs: 2g | Fiber: 2g | Protein: 1g

Rosemary-Garlic Pecans

Prep: 3 minutes | Cook: 30 minutes | Serves 4

Ingredients:

- 1 medium egg white
- 3 tbsp dried rosemary, finely chopped
- 2 tsp garlic salt
- 3 cups pecans

Instructions:

1. Preheat the oven to 120°C.
2. Whisk the egg white, rosemary, and garlic salt in a medium bowl. Add the pecans and toss to coat. Spread in an even layer on a large-rimmed baking sheet.
3. Roast the pecans, stirring every 15 minutes, until dry, about 45 minutes.
4. Let it cool, then enjoy.

Nutrition Facts (Per Serving): Calories: 175 | Fat:18g | Carbs: 4g | Fiber: 3g | Protein: 3g

Salmon Cakes with Potato and Fire Roasted Corn Salsa

Prep: 10 minutes | Cook: 30 minutes | Serves 4

Ingredients:

- 2 medium russet potatoes, peeled and quartered
- 1 can salmon (170g), drained
- 1 small onion, chopped or grated
- 1 egg
- ¼ cup flour
- ¼ cup fresh dill, chopped
- ¼ tsp salt
- ¼ tsp pepper
- 6 tbsp Extra-virgin olive oil

For the Salsa:

- 2 large ears corn, shucked
- 1 medium red pepper, diced
- 2 Jalapeño, diced
- 12 cherry tomatoes, cut in half
- 3 tbsp cider vinegar
- Salt and pepper, to taste

Instructions:

1. Roast the corn cobs on a grill, shave the corn grains off the cob and put them in a bowl.
2. Mix the corn grains with the rest of the salsa ingredients.
3. For the salmon cakes, boil peeled potatoes until they soften, then drain. Mash the potatoes with a fork.
4. Flake the salmon in a large bowl using a fork. Add in onion, egg, flour, dill, salt, pepper, and potatoes and mix well.
5. Make 12 patties.
6. Heat olive oil in a frying pan and fry until golden brown for 5 minutes per side.
7. Serve the salmon cakes with fire-roasted salsa.

Nutritional Facts (Per Serving): Calories: 441 | Fat: 25g | Carbs: 40g | Fiber: 4g | Protein: 17g

Carrot Cake Energy Bites

Prep: 5 minutes | Cook: 10 minutes | Serves 4

Instructions:

- 1 cup pitted dates
- ½ cup old-fashioned rolled oats
- ¼ cup chopped pecans
- ¼ cup chia seeds

- 2 medium carrots, finely chopped
- 1 tsp vanilla extract
- ¾ tsp ground cinnamon
- ½ tsp ground ginger
- ¼ tsp ground turmeric
- ¼ tsp salt
- Pinch of ground pepper

Instructions:

1. Blend all dates, oats, pecans, and chia seeds in a food processor until it is a well-combined mixture.
2. Add carrots, vanilla, cinnamon, ginger, turmeric, salt, and pepper; process until all ingredients are well chopped and a paste begins to form.
3. Make the mixture into balls using 1 tbsp. Each.
4. Refrigerate and enjoy

Nutrition Facts (Per Serving): Calories: 48 | Fat: 2g | Carbs: 8g | Fiber: 2g | Protein: 1g

Pistachio & Peach Toast

Prep: 5 minutes | Cook: 2 minutes | Serves 1

Ingredients:

- 1 tbsp part-skim ricotta cheese
- 1 tsp honey, divided
- ⅛ tsp cinnamon
- 1 slice 100% whole-wheat bread, toasted
- ½ medium peach, sliced
- 1 tbsp chopped pistachios

Instructions:

1. Mix the ricotta, ½ tsp honey, and cinnamon in a small bowl.
2. Spread the ricotta mixture on toast and top with peach and pistachios. Drizzle with the remaining 1/2 tsp honey.

Nutritional Facts (Per Serving): Calories: 193 | Fat: 6g | Carbs: 29g | Fiber: 4g | Protein: 8g

Spanakopita

Prep: 20 minutes | Cook: 30 minutes | Serves 3

Ingredients:

- 450g chopped spinach,
- 2 bunches flat-leaf parsley, finely chopped
- 1 large yellow onion, finely chopped
- 2 garlic cloves, minced

- 2 tbsp Extra-virgin olive oil
- 4 Eggs
- 295g quality feta cheese, crumbled
- 2 tsp dried dill weed
- Freshly-ground black pepper
- 1 (450g) package phyllo dough
- 1 cup Extra-virgin olive oil

Instructions:

1. Preheat the oven to 160°C.
2. Rinse and drain the spinach.
3. Mix the spinach and the remaining filling ingredients in a bowl until all is well combined.
4. Brush the bottom of a 9½" X 13" dish with olive oil.
5. Cover the sides of the baking dish with two sheets of phyllo. Brush with olive oil. Add on another two phyllo sheets and brush them with olive oil. Continue till two-thirds of the phyllo is used up.
6. Spread the spinach and feta filling evenly on the phyllo crust. Cover with two more sheets, brushing with olive oil.
7. Continue this until the phyllo is used up.
8. Brush the folded sides using the remaining olive oil. Ensure the Spanakopita is cut ONLY PART-WAY through into squares.
9. Bake in the oven for 1 hour or until the phyllo crust is crisp and golden brown. Cut into squares and enjoy.

Nutritional Facts (Per Serving): Calories: 393 | Fat: 20.6g | Carbs: 38.8g | Fiber: 6g | Protein: 17g

Tuna Deviled Eggs

Prep: 15 minutes | Cook: 15 minutes | Serves 4

Ingredients:

- 12 eggs
- 1 (125g) can tuna, drained and flaked
- 2 tsp sweet pickle relish, drained
- 1 tsp mustard
- ¼ tsp white sugar (Optional)
- ⅛ tsp onion powder
- Mayonnaise
- salt and pepper to taste
- Paprika

Instructions:

1. Boil the eggs, remove from heat, and let eggs sit in hot water for 15 minutes. Peel the eggs under cold running water.
2. Cut the eggs in half lengthwise; take the yolks and place in a bowl.

3. Mash the egg yolks with a fork, adding the tuna, pickle relish, mustard, sugar, and onion powder, and mayonnaise until mixture is creamy but remains firm; season with salt and pepper.
4. Sit the egg whites cut side up and spoon the tuna mixture into egg white halves; sprinkle with paprika.

Nutritional Facts (Per Serving): Calories: 213 | Fat: 15g | Carbs: 3g | Fiber: 0g | Protein: 18g

French Tuna Rillettes

Prep: 2 minutes | Cook: 10 minutes | Serves 2

Ingredients:

- 1 can (195g) wild-caught tuna,
- 1 shallot, finely chopped
- 2 tbsp chives, chopped
- 1 tbsp sour cream
- 1 tbsp cream cheese
- 2 tbsp heavy cream
- ½ tbsp extra-virgin olive oil
- ½ tsp mustard
- Salt and pepper

Instructions:

1. Drain the tuna completely, then mash till it looks like tiny filaments. Place it in a bowl and mix it with all other ingredients.
2. Serve with crackers or with bread slices.

Nutritional Facts (Per Serving): Calories: 194 | Fat: 13g | Carbs: 3g | Fiber: 1g | Protein: 15g

Peanut Butter Sesame Seed Balls

Prep: 10 minutes | Cook: 10 minutes | Serves 7

Ingredients:

- 2 cups rolled oats
- 1 cup natural peanut butter
- ½ cup honey
- ¼ cup mini chocolate chips
- ¼ cup unsweetened shredded coconut

Instructions:

1. Pour the oats, peanut butter, honey, chocolate chips, and coconut into a medium bowl and mix well.

2. Using a 1-tbsp measure, roll the mixture into balls.
3. Roll in sesame seeds and serve.

Nutritional Facts (Per Serving): Calories: 174 | Fat: 9g | Carbs: 18g | Fiber: 2g | Protein: 4g

Greek Yogurt Breakfast Parfait

Prep: 10 minutes | Cook: 0 minutes | Serves 8

Ingredients:

- 4 cups nonfat plain Greek yogurt
- 1 cup granular sucralose sweetener
- 1½ tsp vanilla extract
- 2 cups granola cereal
- 8 cups frozen mixed fruit

Instructions:

1. Mix the yogurt, sweetener, and vanilla extract in a big bowl thoroughly.
2. Place 1 cup of frozen fruit in plastic cups and top it with ½ cup of yogurt mixture.
3. Top off finally with 1/4 cup granola before eating.

Nutritional Facts (Per Serving): Calories: 359 | Fat: 8g | Carbs: 61g | Fiber: 4g | Protein: 14g

White Corn Balls

Prep: 13 minutes | Cook: 0 minutes | Serves 4

Ingredients:

- 1 ½ cups quick oats
- 1 cup roasted white corn flour
- 1 tsp ground cinnamon
- 1 tsp salt
- ½ cup natural peanut butter
- ¼ cup unsweetened applesauce
- 2 tbsp pure maple syrup
- 2 tbsp water
- 2 tbsp honey
- 1 tsp vanilla extract
- ½ cup unsweetened coconut flakes,
- ½ cup dried raisins and/or currants
- ½ cup unsalted roasted pecans, almonds, walnuts and/or hazelnuts

Instructions:

1. Combine the oats, corn flour, cinnamon, and salt in a medium bowl.

Mix in peanut butter, applesauce, maple syrup, 2 tbsp water, honey and vanilla. Gently stir in coconut flakes, dried fruit, and nuts.
2. Roll the mixture into 1-inch balls, using 1 tbsp to make each.

Nutritional Facts (Per Serving): Calories: 77g | Fat: 4g | Carbs: 9g | Fiber: 1g | Protein: 2g

Muhammara (Roasted Red Pepper and Walnut Dip)

Prep: 5 minutes | Cook: 30 minutes | Serves 6

Ingredients:

- 2 red bell peppers
- tbsp Extra-virgin Olive Oil divided
- 110g shelled toasted walnuts
- 1 garlic clove roughly chopped
- 2½ tbsp tomato paste
- ¾ cup bread crumbs
- 2 tbsp pomegranate molasses
- 1 tsp Aleppo pepper
- 1/2 tsp sugar
- 1 tsp sumac
- 1/2 tsp salt
- 1/2 tsp cayenne pepper

Instructions:

- Preheat the oven to 110°C.
- Brush the bell peppers with olive oil, placing them in a lightly oiled oven-safe pan. Roast the peppers in the oven for 30 minutes, turning them over twice.
- Take the peppers out of the oven and place in a bowl. Cover with plastic wrap for a few minutes and peel to remove the seeds when cool.
- Slice the peppers into small strips.
- Combine the roasted red pepper strips with 3 tbsp Extra-virgin olive oil, garlic, walnuts, tomato paste, bread crumbs, pomegranate molasses, Aleppo pepper, sugar, sumac, salt, and cayenne in a food processor.
- Blend into a smooth paste and transfer to a serving bowl.

Nutritional Facts (Per Serving): Calories: 201 | Fat: 22.6g | Carbs: 21.5g | Fiber: 3.1g | Protein: 5.5g

Tortilla De Patata (Spanish Potato Omelets)

Prep: 15 minutes | Cook: 15 minutes | Serves 4

Ingredients:

- 3 medium potatoes
- 1 onion, diced
- 1 cup Extra-virgin olive oil
- ¾ tsp salt
- ¼ tsp black pepper
- Eggs
- ¼ cup milk

Instructions:

1. Wash and peel potatoes, thinly slicing them using a grater.
2. Heat oil and add onions to oil, then add potatoes.
3. Whisk the eggs with salt, pepper, and milk.
4. Turn the potatoes every few minutes and remove when they are brown and tender.
5. Add potatoes and onion to bowl with whisked eggs and milk.
6. Pour some oil into a heated pan and go in with the egg, potato and milk mixture into the pan.
7. Cover the pan with a plate bigger than the pan to flip the tortilla. Flip the pan with the plate held tightly to the pan.
8. Remove once the egg is firm and cooked through. Serve

Nutritional Facts (Per Serving): Calories: 461 | Fat: 33g | Carbs: 32g | Fiber: 4g | Protein: 11g

Crunchy Granola

Prep: 10 minutes | Cook: 30 minutes | Serves 6

Ingredients:

- 3 ¾ cups rolled oats
- ½ cup chopped almonds
- ¼ cup dried unsweetened coconut
- ¼ cup sesame seeds
- 2 tsp ground cinnamon
- ¼ tsp salt
- 3 large egg whites
- 1 tsp vanilla extract (Optional)

Instructions:

1. Preheat the oven to 110°C.
2. Empty oats, almonds, coconut, sesame seeds, cinnamon, and salt in a bowl.
3. Whisk egg whites until stiff peaks form, then beat in vanilla extract. Fold egg whites into the oat mixture; spread onto the baking pan lined with parchment.

4. Bake in the preheated oven until granola is crispy for 1 hour, stirring every 20 minutes.

Nutritional Facts (Per Serving): Calories: 332 | Fat: 15g | Carbs: 40g | Fiber: 8g | Protein: 12g

Savory Date & Pistachio Bites

Prep: 10 minutes | Cook: 0 minutes | Serves 8

Ingredients:

- 2 cups pitted whole dates
- 1 cup raw unsalted shelled pistachios
- 1 cup golden raisins
- 1 tsp ground fennel seeds
- ¼ tsp ground pepper

Instructions:

1. Combine dates, pistachios, raisins, fennel, and pepper in a food processor. Process until finely chopped.
2. Form into about 32 balls, using 1 tbsp each.

Nutritional Facts (Per Serving): Calories: 68 | Fat: 2g | Carbs: 13g | Fiber: 1g | Protein: 1g

Zucchini Fritters with Feta, Cheddar, Mint and Parsley

Prep: 10 minutes | Cook: 25 minutes | Serves 4

Ingredients:

- Medium zucchinis, grated
- 1 cup onion, grated
- 1/2 tbsp salt
- 4-6 eggs
- 1 cup cheddar cheese, grated
- ½ cup feta cheese, grated
- 3-4 cups bread crumbs
- ½ cup fresh mint leaves, chopped
- 1 cup fresh parsley, chopped
- ¼ tsp freshly ground pepper
- 1 cup Olive oil for frying

Instructions:

1. Place the grated zucchini, onion, and salt in a colander, and drain for 15-20 minutes.
2. In a large bowl, add 2 beaten eggs, cheddar and feta, zucchini mixture, 1 cup bread crumbs, mint, parsley, and

ground pepper. Mix the ingredients with a fork. Add breadcrumbs until fritters can be formed with your hands.
3. Whisk two eggs in a small bowl.
4. In another bowl, add 1 cup breadcrumbs.
5. Heat 1 cup of olive oil in a frying pan.
6. Brush the fritters with eggs and then bread crumbs.
7. Fry in olive oil. Drain on paper towels.

Nutritional Facts (Per Serving): Calories: 436 | Fat: 31g | Carbs: 29g | Fiber: 3g | Protein: 12g

Kalamata Olive Tapenade

Prep: 15 minutes | Cook: 2 minutes | Serves 8

Ingredients:

- 3 cloves garlic, peeled
- 1 cup pitted kalamata olives
- 3 tbsp chopped fresh parsley
- 2 tbsp capers
- 2 tbsp lemon juice
- 2 tbsp olive oil
- salt and pepper to taste

Instructions:

1. Mince garlic cloves, olives, parsley, capers, lemon juice, and olive oil in a blender until the mixture is fine.
2. Season with salt and pepper.

Nutritional Facts (Per Serving): Calories: 81 | Fat: 8g | Carbs: 3g | Fiber: 0g | Protein: 1g

Greek Salad Skewers

Prep: 10 minutes | Cook: 2 minutes | Serves 6

Ingredients:

- 170g creamy feta cheese, cut into 12 cubes
- ½ English cucumber, sliced into half-moons
- 1 small green pepper, cored, cut into 12 square pieces
- 12 cherry or grape tomatoes

- 12 pitted Kalamata olives

For the Dressing:

- 1 garlic clove, minced
- ½ lime, juice of
- 1 tbsp red wine vinegar
- 1 tbsp Extra-virgin olive oil
- Kosher salt and black pepper
- 1 tsp dried oregano

Instructions:

1. Skewer a feta cube, a slice of cucumber, a piece of green pepper, one cherry tomato, and one kalamata olive at the top. Do this for 10 to 12 skewers.
2. Mix the garlic, lime juice, olive oil, red wine vinegar, kosher salt, black pepper, and dried oregano.
3. Arrange the skewers on a serving platter and pour the dressing over. Enjoy.

Nutritional Facts (Per Serving): Calories: 122 | Fat: 9.6g | Carbs: 5.3g | Fiber: 1.3g | Protein: 4.8g

Everything-Bagel Crispy Chickpeas

Prep: 10 minutes | Cook: 30 minutes | Serves 6

Ingredients:

- 2 (425g) cans unsalted chickpeas, rinsed
- 3 tbsp extra-virgin olive oil
- 2 tbsp everything bagel seasoning

Instructions:

1. Preheat the oven to 200°C.
2. Line a baking sheet with paper towels.
3. Remove the chickpea skins.
4. Toss the chickpeas drizzled with oil in a large bowl.
5. Spread in an even layer on the hot baking sheet. Roast till for 30 minutes.
6. Meanwhile, grind everything bagel seasoning in a spice grinder. When the chickpeas are done, sprinkle the hot chickpeas with the ground seasoning.
7. Let it cool completely for 10 minutes; enjoy!

Nutritional Facts (Per Serving): Calories: 220 | Fat: 8g | Carbs: 25g | Fiber: 6g | Protein: 9g

Apple with Cinnamon Almond Butter

Prep: 5 minutes | Cook: 0 minutes | Serves 2

Ingredients:

- 1 medium apple
- 1 tbsp smooth almond butter
- Pinch of ground cinnamon

Instructions:

1. Divide apple into eight slices. Spread each slice with a little almond butter and sprinkle some cinnamon.

Nutritional Facts (Per Serving): Calories: 193 | Fat: 9g | Carbs: 28g | Fiber: 6g | Protein: 4g

Peanut Butter Energy Balls

Prep: 20 minutes | Cook: 0 minutes | Serves 7

Ingredients:

- 2 cups rolled oats
- 1 cup natural peanut butter
- ½ cup honey
- ¼ cup mini chocolate chips
- ¼ cup unsweetened shredded coconut

Instructions:

1. Combine oats, peanut butter, honey, chocolate chips, and coconut in a medium bowl; stir well.
2. Measure 1 tbsp scoops of the mixture and roll into balls.

Nutritional Facts (Per Serving): Calories: 174 | Fat: 9g | Carbs: 18g | Fiber: 4g | Protein: 4g

Greek Fava

Prep: 10 minutes | Cook: 25 minutes | Serves 4

Ingredients:

- 225g dried yellow split peas
- 1 medium brown onion, chopped
- 1 small clove garlic, crushed
- 1/2 lemon juice
- 1 tsp olive oil
- Salt and black pepper, to taste

- Paprika and olive oil to garnish

Instructions:

1. Cover the split peas and onions in a saucepan with enough water to cover a few inches above the beans.
2. Boil, then reduce the heat and simmer for 45 minutes, until the peas are thick and soft. Drain excess water off before transferring the peas to a bowl.
3. Mix in the garlic, lemon juice, and oil until it is well blended. Let it cool, then add salt and pepper to taste and garnish with paprika.

Nutritional Facts (Per Serving): Calories: 215 | Fat: 2g | Carbs: 37g | Fiber: 15g | Protein: 14g

Almond Crackers

Prep: 20 minutes | Cook: 15 minutes | Serves 5

Ingredients:

- 1 cup almond flour
- 2 tbsp finely chopped walnuts
- 1 ½ tsp flax seed meal
- ½ tsp salt
- 2 tbsp water
- 1 ½ tsp olive oil

Instructions:

1. Set the oven to 175°C. Line a baking pan with parchment paper.
2. Mix almond flour, walnuts, flax seed meal, and salt in a bowl. Add water and olive oil, mixing until the dough is moist and holds together.
3. Use a rolling pin to roll the dough into a 1/16-inch-thick rectangle.
4. Cut the sides of the dough, making an even rectangle. Add excess dough to the corners or one end of the rectangle and re-roll to a uniform thickness.
5. Cut the dough into 1" squares without completely detaching the dough.
6. Bake in the preheated oven until the outside edges of the dough are browned, about 15 minutes.
7. Cool the crackers, then break into squares.

Nutritional Facts (Per Serving): Calories: 36 |Fat: 4g | Carbs: 1g | Fiber: 0g | Protein: 1g

Kale Chips

Prep: 10 minutes | Cook: 20 minutes | Serves 6

Ingredients:

- 1 bunch kale
- 1 tbsp olive oil
- 1 tsp flaked sea salt

Instructions:

1. Preheat the oven to 150°C. Line a rimmed baking sheet with parchment paper.
2. Remove kale leaves carefully from the stems, tearing them into bite-sized pieces.
3. Dry the kale using a salad spinner.
4. Drizzle kale leaves with olive oil and spread them out in an even layer on the baking sheet without overlapping, then sprinkle salt.
5. Bake until the edges start to brown but are not burnt, 20 to 30 minutes.

Nutritional Facts (Per Serving): Calories: 58 | Fat 3g | Carbs: 8g | Fiber: 2g | Protein: 3g

Classic Hummus with Pita Bread

Prep: 10 minutes | Cook: 20 minutes | Serves 4

Ingredients:

- 1 cup chickpeas, soaked overnight and drained.
- 3 tbsp tahini
- 2 cloves of garlic
- Extra-virgin olive oil
- 5 cubes of ice
- 2 tbsp lime juice
- Sea salt (as per taste)
- Olive oil
- Parsley
- Pomegranate
- Za'atar
- Sumac
- Paprika
- Pita Bread

Instructions:

1. Boil the chickpeas until soft and drain.
2. Reserve some drained water and peel the chickpea skins.

3. Blend the peeled chickpeas along with all of the other ingredients for the hummus (tahini, garlic, ice cubes, lime juice, salt, and olive oil), as well as a few tbsp of the reserved chickpea water.
4. Blend to the desired consistency.
5. Spread the hummus on a plate and garnish with fresh parsley, za'atar, and a scattering of pomegranates.
6. Enjoy with the pita bread.

Nutritional Facts (Per Serving): Calories: 515 | Fat: 36g | Carbs: 39g | Fiber: 8g | Protein: 21.5g

Greek Stuffed Grape Leaves

Prep: 20 minutes | Cook: 30 minutes | Serves 12

Ingredients:

- 1 (450g) jar grape leaves in brine (about 60 to 70 leaves)
- 1½ cup short grain rice, soaked then drained
- Extra-virgin olive oil
- 1 large yellow onion, finely chopped
- 12 oz lean ground beef
- Kosher salt
- Black pepper
- 1 tsp allspice
- ½ tsp cumin
- ½ cup each chopped fresh parsley, fresh dill, and fresh mint
- 1 to 2 tomatoes sliced into rounds
- Low-sodium chicken broth
- Juice of 2 lemons

Instructions:

1. Soak the rice in plenty of water for 20 minutes until the grains break easily. Drain well.
2. Heat up 1 tbsp of Extra-virgin olive oil.
3. Mix in onions and cook briefly until it's translucent.
4. Add the meat and cook till fully browned. Season with kosher salt, pepper, and spices. Take this off the heat.
5. Mix the meat, drained rice, and fresh herbs in a bowl. Season lightly with kosher salt. Add a lot of olive oil, and mix thoroughly.
6. Lightly brush the bottom of a large cooking pot with the olive oil. Place a few grape leaves in the bottom. Top with sliced tomatoes.
7. Put the filling into the center of the rough side of the leaf, then roll like rolling spring rolls. Repeat with other grape leaves.
8. Place the grape leaves in a row in the prepared pot. Boil the broth and pour over the grape leaves, covering them a bit.

9. Cover the pot and cook on medium heat for 30 minutes until the liquid has been absorbed. Uncover and squeeze in 2 lemons. Cover again and simmer on low heat for 45 more minutes.
10. Remove grape leaves from heat. Allow to rest uncovered for 20 to 30 minutes before serving.

Nutritional Facts (Per Serving): Calories: 125 | Fat: 5g | Carbs: 14g | Fiber: 2g | Protein: 8g

MEDITERRANEAN SOUP RECIPES

White Bean Soup with Escarole

Prep: 10 minutes | Cook: 30 minutes | Serves 8

Ingredients:

- 1 tbsp olive oil
- 1 small onion, chopped
- garlic cloves, minced
- 3 cans (410g each) reduced-sodium chicken broth
- 1 can (410g) diced tomatoes, undrained
- 1/2 tsp Italian seasoning
- 1/4 tsp crushed red pepper flakes
- 1 cup uncooked whole wheat orzo pasta
- 1 bunch escarole or spinach, coarsely chopped (about 8 cups)
- 1 can (425g) cannellini beans, rinsed and drained
- 1/4 cup shredded Parmesan cheese

Instructions:

1. Heat some olive oil over medium heat using a Dutch oven.
2. Stir in the onion and garlic and cook until tender.
3. Pour in the broth, tomatoes, Italian seasoning, and pepper flakes, and bring to a boil.
4. Reduce heat and let it simmer uncovered for 15 minutes.
5. Pour in the escarole and orzo and mix.
6. Return this to boil for 14 minutes until the orzo is tender.
7. Add the cannellini and heat it through, stirring in intervals. Sprinkle the servings with cheese.

Nutritional Facts (Per Serving): Calories: 174 | Fat: 3g | Carbs: 28g | Fiber: 8g | Protein: 9g

Chicken Meatball Soup

Prep: 15 minutes | Cook: 25 minutes | Serves 6

Ingredients:

- 455g ground chicken
- ½ cup panko bread crumbs
- 1 large egg
- Grated parmesan cheese

- ¼ cup finely chopped fresh parsley
- 1 cup diced white onion
- ½ cup diced carrots
- ½ cup diced celery
- 4 cloves garlic, minced
- 8 cups chicken stock
- 1 dried bay leaf
- 1 cup dried orzo pasta
- 4 cups roughly chopped Swiss chard
- Kosher salt
- Black pepper
- Olive oil
- 1 tbsp lemon juice

Instructions:

1. Combine the ground chicken, bread crumbs, egg, parmesan, garlic, parsley, salt, and pepper into a bowl and mix well. Roll into 1-inch meatballs.
2. Heat some olive oil in a large pot and sear the meatballs until they're golden brown on all sides, then remove.
3. Still using the same pot, heat a tbsp of oil and fry the garlic, onion, carrot, and celery till tender.
4. Add the chicken stock and bay leaf and boil.
5. Once boiling, add the orzo and meatballs. Simmer for 8 minutes until the orzo is tender.
6. Add the Swiss chard and cook till the chard wilts before adding the parmesan cheese.
7. Season to taste with salt and pepper. Add the lemon juice and simmer for 4 minutes.
8. Serve.

Nutritional Facts (Per Serving): Calories: 435 | Fat: 18g | Carbs: 47g | Fiber: 4g | Protein: 35g

Greek Bean Soup (Fasolada)

Prep: 10 minutes | Cook: 20 minutes | Serves 6

Ingredients:

- Extra-virgin Olive Oil
- 1 large yellow onion, chopped
- ½ tsp salt
- ½ tsp black pepper
- 2 garlic cloves, minced
- celery ribs, chopped
- 1 tsp dried oregano
- 1 dried bay leaf
- 4½ cups chicken broth (or vegetable broth)
- 3 (425g) cans cannellini beans, drained and rinsed
- ½ tsp ground cumin

- ¼ tsp sweet paprika
- ¼ tsp cayenne pepper
- 1 lemon, zested and juiced
- ½ cup chopped fresh parsley leaves

Instructions

1. Heat 2 tbsp of Extra-virgin olive oil in a heavy pot.
2. Stir in the chopped onion, salt, and pepper, and cook for about 4 minutes. Mix in the garlic, celery, bay leaf, and oregano. Cook for 5 more minutes.
3. Add broth, cannellini beans, cumin, paprika, and cayenne pepper. Raise the heat and bring to a quick boil for 3 minutes. Lower the heat and let simmer for 10 minutes.
4. Scoop 2 cups of the soup into a small food processor. Blend and return to the cooking pot. Simmer for another 5 minutes. Remove from heat.
5. Off heat, stir in about 1/3 cup Extra-virgin olive oil, lemon zest, lemon juice, and parsley.
6. Serve with your favorite bread.

Nutritional Facts (Per Serving): Calories: 409 | Fat: 8.7g | Carbs: 63.3g | Fiber: | Protein: 22g

Seafood Soup

Prep: 10 minutes | Cook: 30 minutes | Serves 6

Ingredients:

- 1 tbsp olive oil
- 1 small onion, chopped
- 1 small green pepper, chopped
- 2 medium carrots, chopped
- 1 garlic clove, minced
- 1 can (425g) tomato sauce
- 1 can (412g) diced tomatoes, undrained
- ¾ cup white wine or chicken broth
- 1 bay leaf
- ½ tsp dried oregano
- ¼ tsp dried basil
- ¼ tsp pepper
- 340g salmon fillets, skinned and cut into 3/4-inch cubes
- 225g uncooked medium shrimp, peeled and deveined
- 2 tbsp minced fresh parsley

Instructions:

- Heat some olive oil in a large saucepan.
- Add in onion and green pepper; cook until tender.
- Add carrots and garlic; cook for another 3 minutes, then stir in tomato sauce, tomatoes, wine, and seasonings and boil. Reduce heat and let it simmer, covered for 30 minutes.
- Stir in salmon, shrimp, and parsley. Cook for 10 minutes more until fish flakes easily with a fork and shrimp turn pink. Discard bay leaf.

Nutritional Facts (Per Serving): Calories: 213 | Fat: 9g | Carbs: 5g | Fiber: 3g | Protein: 18g

Italian White Bean Soup

Prep: 10 minutes | Cook: 30 minutes | Serves 4

Ingredients:

- 1 tbsp vegetable oil
- 1 onion, chopped
- 1 rib celery, chopped
- 1 clove garlic, minced
- 2 (425g) cans white cannellini beans, rinsed and drained
- 1 (397g) can chicken broth
- ¼ tsp ground black pepper
- ⅛ tsp dried thyme
- 2 cups water
- 1 bunch fresh spinach, rinsed and thinly sliced
- 1 tbsp lemon juice

Instructions:

- Heat up some oil in a soup pot and stir in onion and celery; cook until tender, then add garlic and cook for 30 seconds, continually stirring.
- Stir in beans, chicken broth, pepper, thyme, and 2 cups water. Bring to a boil, reduce heat, and simmer for 15 minutes.
- Take out 2 cups of bean and vegetable mixture from soup; set aside.
- Blend the remaining soup using a blender at low speed until smooth.
- Pour blended soup back into pot; stir in reserved beans.
- Bring soup to a boil, occasionally stirring. Stir in spinach until it is wilted, about 1 minute.
- Stir in lemon juice and remove from heat. Serve soup with freshly grated Parmesan cheese on top.

Nutrition Facts (Per Serving): Calories: 245 | Fat: 5g | Carbs: 38g | Fiber: 11g | Protein: 12g

Lemony Greek Chickpea Soup

Prep: 10 minutes | Cook: 20 minutes | Serves 6

Ingredients:

- 2 Tbsp. extra-virgin olive oil
- 1 ½ cups finely chopped yellow or sweet onion
- 3/4 cup finely chopped carrots
- 1/2 cup finely chopped celery
- 2 (2-inch) strips lemon peel, plus 1/4 cup fresh lemon juice, divided
- garlic cloves, minced
- cups lower-sodium vegetable broth
- 2 (440g) cans chickpeas, rinsed and drained
- 3/4 cup dry orzo pasta (regular or whole-wheat)
- 1 tsp. kosher salt
- 1 tsp. black pepper
- 1 tsp. dried oregano
- 2 large whole eggs plus two egg yolks
- 3 handfuls roughly chopped or shredded kale
- 2 Tbsp. Finely chopped fresh dill

Instructions:

1. Heat oil in a Dutch oven and add the onion, carrots, celery, and lemon peel. Cook for 10 minutes, then add garlic; cook one more minute.
2. Add broth and increase heat to bring the mixture to a boil. Once boiling, add chickpeas, orzo, salt, pepper, and oregano. Then simmer the soup uncovered until the orzo is al dente. Lower heat and remove ¾ cup hot broth from the soup. Set aside.
3. Whisk whole eggs, egg yolks, and lemon and slowly stream hot broth into the egg mixture.
4. Slowly pour the egg-broth mixture back into the pot of soup. Add kale and cook on low heat for 5 minutes.
5. Sprinkle in dill and serve.

Nutritional Facts (Per Serving): Calories: 340 Fat: 11g | Carbs: 47g | Fiber: 8g | Protein: 15g

Arborio Rice and White Bean Soup

Prep: 5 minutes | Cook: 25 minutes | Serves 4

Ingredients:

- 1 tbsp olive oil
- garlic cloves, minced
- ¾ cup uncooked arborio rice
- 1 carton (907g) vegetable broth
- ¾ tsp dried basil
- ½ tsp dried thyme
- ¼ tsp dried oregano
- 1 package (453g) frozen broccoli-cauliflower blend
- 1 can (425g) cannellini beans, rinsed and drained
- 2 cups fresh baby spinach

Instructions:

1. In a large saucepan, heat oil over medium heat; sauté garlic for 1 minute.
2. Stir in rice and cook for 2 minutes. Then stir in the broth and herbs and let boil. Reduce heat and simmer until rice is al dente.
3. Pour in the frozen vegetables and beans; cook until rice is tender.
4. Stir in spinach until wilted and remove from heat.
5. Serve.

Nutrition Facts (Per Serving): Calories: 303 | Fat: 4g | Fiber: 6g | Protein: 9g

Pea Stew

Prep: 10 minutes | Cook: 25 minutes | Serves 4

Ingredients:

- 1 carrot, cubed
- 1 yellow onion, chopped
- 1½ tbsp olive oil
- 1 celery stick, chopped
- Garlic cloves, minced
- 2 cups yellow peas
- 1½ tsp cumin, ground
- 1 tsp sweet paprika
- ¼ tsp chili powder
- Black pepper
- ¼ tsp cinnamon powder
- ½ cup tomatoes, chopped
- Juice of ½ lemon
- 1-quart low-sodium veggie stock
- 1 tbsp chives, chopped

Instructions:

1. Heat a pot with the olive oil on medium heat, and stir in carrots, onion, and celery, cooking this for 5-6 minutes.

2. Add garlic, peas, cumin, paprika, chili powder, pepper, cinnamon, tomatoes, lemon juice, peas, and stock. Simmer over medium heat for 20 minutes; add chives.
3. Serve.

Nutritional Facts (Per Serving): Calories: 22 | Fat: 6g | Carbs: 14g | Fiber: | Protein: 9g

Summer Squash & White Bean Soup

Prep: 10 minutes | Cook: 20 minutes | Serves 4

Ingredients:

- 2 tbsp olive oil
- 1 medium yellow onion, diced small
- 4 garlic cloves, minced
- 1 tbsp fresh oregano, minced
- ½ tsp fine sea salt
- ¼ tsp black pepper
- 4 cups low-sodium vegetable broth
- 5-inch Parmigiano-Reggiano cheese
- 2 cups summer squash, seeded and diced medium
- 2 cups zucchini, diced medium
- 1 cup cooked navy or cannellini beans
- ½ cup fresh basil, chopped
- ¼ cup fresh parsley, chopped

Instructions:

- Heat some olive oil in a large pot and sauté the onions for 5 minutes. Then, add the garlic, oregano, salt, and pepper and keep sautéing for 3 more minutes.
- Stir in the vegetable broth and cheese rind and gently simmer.
- Finally, mix in the summer squash, zucchini, white beans, basil, and parsley and simmer until the squash is tender.
- Season with more salt and pepper if needed, and serve hot.

Nutritional Facts (Per Serving): Calories: 190 | Fat: 9g | Carbs: 19g | Fiber: 7g | Protein: 10g

Eggplant Stew

Prep: 10 minutes | Cook: 20 minutes | Serves 4

Ingredients:

- ½ tsp cumin seeds
- 1 tbsp coriander seeds
- ½ tsp mustard seeds

- 1 tbsp olive oil
- 1 tbsp ginger, grated
- 2 garlic cloves, minced
- 1 green chili pepper, chopped
- cinnamon powder
- ½ tsp cardamom, ground
- ½ tsp turmeric powder
- 1 tsp lime juice
- baby eggplants, cubed
- 1 cup low-sodium veggie stock
- 1 tbsp cilantro, chopped

Instructions:

1. Heat a pot with the oil over medium-high heat; add cumin, coriander, and mustard seeds, stir and cook them for 5 minutes.
2. Add ginger, garlic, chili, cinnamon, cardamom, and turmeric, stir and cook for 5 minutes more.
3. Add lime juice, eggplants, and stock, stir, cover, and cook over medium heat for 15 minutes.
4. Add cilantro, stir, divide into bowls and, serve for lunch.

Nutritional Facts (Per Serving): Calories: 270 | Fat: 4g | Carbs: 12g | Fiber: | Protein: 9g

Chicken Spinach Soup with Fresh Pesto

Prep: 10 minutes | Cook: 20 minutes | Serves 5

Ingredients:

- Extra-virgin olive oil, divided
- ½ cup carrot
- 227g boneless, skinless chicken breast
- 1 large clove garlic, minced
- 3 cups reduced-sodium chicken broth
- 1½ tsp dried marjoram
- Baby spinach, coarsely chopped
- 1 (425g) can cannellini beans or great northern beans, rinsed
- ¼ cup grated Parmesan cheese
- ⅓ cup lightly packed fresh basil leaves
- Freshly ground pepper, to taste
- ¾ cup plain or herbed multigrain croutons for garnish

Instructions:

1. Heat some oil in a large saucepan or Dutch oven over medium-high heat. Add carrot and chicken; cook until the

chicken begins to brown, 3 minutes. Add garlic and cook, stirring, for 1 minute more. Stir in broth and marjoram; bring to a boil over high heat.

2. Transfer the chicken pieces to a clean cutting board to cool. Add spinach and beans to the pot and bring to a gentle boil. Cook for 5 minutes to blend the flavors.
3. For the pesto, mix the remaining 1 tbsp oil, parmesan, and basil in a food processor. Pulse until a coarse paste forms, adding a little water as necessary.
4. Cut the chicken into bite-size pieces. Stir the chicken and pesto into the pot. Season with pepper. Heat until hot. Garnish with croutons, if desired.

Nutritional Facts (Per Serving): Calories: 227 | Fat: 9g | Carbs: 18g | Fiber: 6g | Protein: 19g

Jackfruit And Chili Stew

Prep: 10 minutes | Cook: 25 minutes | Serves 4

Ingredients:

- 1.1kg canned jackfruit
- 398g canned red chili puree
- 1 yellow onion, chopped
- garlic cloves, minced
- 1 tbsp olive oil
- 8 cups low-sodium veggie stock
- 1 tbsp oregano, chopped
- 1 tbsp cilantro, chopped

Instructions:

1. Heat a pot with the oil over medium-high heat, add onion and garlic, stir, and cook for 4-5 minutes.
2. Add jackfruit, chili puree, and stock, stir, cover, and cook over medium heat for 15 minutes.
3. Add oregano and cilantro, stir, cook for 5 minutes more, divide into bowls and serve.

Nutritional Facts (Per Serving): Calories: 263 | Fat: 6g | Carbs: 13g | Fiber: | Protein: 11g

Vegetable Ravioli Soup

Prep: 5 minutes | Cook: 25 minutes | Serves 4

Ingredients:

- 1 tbsp extra-virgin olive oil
- 2 cups frozen bell pepper and onion mix, thawed and diced
- 2 cloves garlic, minced
- 1/4 tsp crushed red pepper, or to taste (optional)
- 1 (794g) can crushed tomatoes, preferably fire-roasted
- 1 (425g) can vegetable broth or reduced-sodium chicken broth
- 1 ½ cups hot water
- 1 tsp dried basil or marjoram
- 255g fresh cheese (or meat) ravioli, preferably whole-wheat
- 2 cups diced zucchini
- Freshly ground pepper to taste

Instructions:

1. Pour some oil into a Dutch oven over medium heat. Add pepper-onion mix, garlic, and crushed red pepper and cook, stirring, for 1 minute.
2. Add tomatoes, broth, water, and basil; bring to a rolling boil over high heat. Add ravioli and cook for 3 minutes less than the package directions. Add zucchini; return to a boil. Cook until the zucchini is crisp-tender, about 3 minutes. Season with pepper.

Nutritional Facts (Per Serving): Calories: 261 | Fat: 8g | Carbs: 33g | | Protein: 11g

MEDITERRANEAN SALADS RECIPES

Mediterranean Edamame & Herb Salad

Prep: 10 minutes | Cook: 5 minutes | Serves 2

Ingredients:

- 150g Shelled Edamame or fresh
- 240g Cherry tomatoes, halved
- ½ cucumber, diced
- 60ml red onions, finely chopped
- 60ml fresh mint leaves, chopped
- 60ml fresh parsley, chopped
- 60g crumbled goat cheese
- 4 tbsp pine nuts, toasted

For the Dressing:

- 2 tbsp extra-virgin olive oil
- 1 tbsp lemon juice
- 1 tsp honey or maple syrup
- Salt and black pepper to taste

Ingredients:

1. Prepare the shelled edamame using package instructions. Drain after and let it cool.
2. Whisk some olive oil, honey or maple syrup, lemon juice, and black pepper in a small bowl to make the dressing.
3. In a larger bowl, mix the cooked edamame, diced cucumber, cherry tomatoes, chopped tomatoes, chopped onions and parsley.
4. Pour the dressing over the salad and toss the salad to combine thoroughly.
5. Sprinkle crumbled goat cheese and pine nuts over the top.

Nutritional Facts (Per Serving): Calories: 300 | Fat: 20g | Carbs: 20g | Fiber: 6g | Protein: 15g

Balela Salad

Prep: 10 minutes | Cook: 10 minutes | Serves 6

Ingredients:

- ½ cup cooked chickpeas, drained and rinsed
- ½ green bell pepper, chopped
- 1 jalapeno, finely chopped
- 2½ cups grape or cherry tomatoes,

- ½ cup sun-dried tomatoes
- 3-5 green onions, chopped
- 1/3 cup pitted Kalamata olives
- ¼ cup pitted green olives
- ½ cup chopped parsley leaves
- ½ cup chopped mint or basil leaves
- ¼ cup Extra-virgin olive oil
- 2 tbsp white wine vinegar
- tbsp lemon juice
- 1 garlic clove, minced
- 1 tsp sumac
- 1/2 tsp Aleppo pepper
- ¼ to ½ tsp crushed red pepper
- Kosher salt
- Black pepper

Instructions:

1. Mix the salad. In a large bowl, mix the chickpeas, bell pepper, jalapeno, tomatoes, green onion, sun-dried tomatoes, olives, and herbs.
2. Whisk the oil, vinegar, salt, lemon juice, garlic, sumac, Aleppo pepper, and red pepper in a separate bowl.
3. Pour the dressing over the salad and mix to coat
4. Serve.

Nutritional Fats (Per Serving): Calories: 303 | Fat: 14g | Carbs: 36.8g | Fiber: 10.5g | Protein: 11g

Greek Pasta Salad

Prep: 20 minutes | Cook: 5 minutes | Serves 4

Ingredients:

- 480g penne pasta, cooked
- 240g cherry tomatoes, halved
- 1 cucumber, diced
- ½ red onions, thinly sliced
- 120g kalamata olives, pitted and sliced
- 120g crumbled feta cheese
- 60g chopped fresh dill
- tbsp chopped fresh dill
- Salt and black pepper to taste
- Extra-virgin olive oil
- 2 tbsp red wine vinegar
- 1 tsp dried oregano
- 1 clove garlic, minced

Ingredients:

1 Boil a large pot with lightly salted water. Stir in penne and return to a boil. Cook pasta uncovered, stirring occasionally, until tender yet firm to

the bite. Rinse with cold water and drain well.
2. Whisk olive oil, vinegar, garlic, lemon juice, oregano, salt, and pepper together in a bowl; set aside.
3. Combine pasta, tomatoes, green and red peppers, onion, cucumber, olives, and feta cheese in a large bowl. Pour vinaigrette over the pasta mixture and mix well.
4. Enjoy!

Nutritional Facts (Per Serving): Calories: 307 | Fat: 24g | Carbs: 19g | Fiber: 2g | Protein: 5g

Mediterranean Chickpea Egg Salad

Prep: 5 minutes | Cook: 10 minutes | Serves 8

Ingredients:

For Dressing:

- 1/2 tsp Dijon mustard
- 1 large lemon, zested and juiced
- 1/3 cup Greek Extra-virgin olive oil
- 1 garlic clove, minced
- 1 tsp sumac
- 1/2 tsp coriander
- 1/2 tsp cayenne pepper
- Salt and pepper

For Egg Salad:

- cans chickpeas, rinsed and drained
- 2 celery ribs, chopped
- 2 Persian cucumbers (or 1/2 seedless English cucumber), diced
- 2 to 3 green onions, trimmed and chopped (both white and green parts)
- 1/2 cup shredded red cabbage
- 2 jalapeno peppers, chopped
- 1/2 cup packed chopped fresh parsley leaves
- 1/2 cup packed chopped fresh mint leaves
- 5 large hard-boiled eggs, sliced

Instructions:

- Mix the dressing ingredients in a bowl and set aside.
- In a large mixing bowl, add all the salad ingredients except the eggs.
- Give the dressing a quick whisk and pour over the salad. Mix to combine.
- Add the sliced eggs, and mix gently again.
- Set aside a few minutes before serving to allow flavors to meld. Enjoy!

Nutritional Facts (Per Serving): Calories: 193 | Fat: 12.9g | Carbs: 12.9g | Fiber: | Protein: 7.9g

Pesto Pasta Salad

Prep: 15 minutes | Cook: 10 minutes | Serves 6

Ingredients:

- 453g whole grain pasta (fusilli, rotini, penne or farfalle)
- 1-pint cherry tomatoes, halved or quartered
- 4 handfuls baby arugula or spinach
- Optional cheese: ½ cup or more crumbled feta cheese
- 1½ cup of cooked chickpeas
- Freshly ground black pepper

For Pesto:

- ½ cup pepitas
- ½ cup packed fresh basil
- ½ cup packed fresh flat-leaf parsley or additional basil
- ¼ cup lemon juice
- 1 clove garlic, roughly chopped
- ½ tsp fine salt
- ⅓ cup extra-virgin olive oil

Instructions

- Boil a large pot of salted water and cook the pasta until al dente. Drain and reserve about ½ cup pasta cooking water, rinse the pasta under cool water to prevent sticking, and transfer to a large serving bowl.
- For the pesto, toast the pepitas using a small pan on medium heat, stirring often. Pour half of the pepitas into a bowl for later.
- Pour the remaining pepitas into a food processor. Add the basil, parsley, lemon juice, and garlic. Make it a smooth paste.
- Mix the pasta and pesto until the pasta is lightly and evenly coated. Add in the cherry tomatoes, arugula, remaining toasted pepitas, and any optional add-ins (cheese, olives, and/or chickpeas).
- Mix again, then season to taste with pepper and serve.

Nutritional Facts (Per Serving): Calories: 343 | Fat: 15g | Carbs: 46g | Fiber: 7g | Protein: 11g

Cannellini Bean Lettuce Wraps

Prep: 10 minutes | Cook: 10 minutes | Serves 4

Ingredients:

- 1 tbsp extra-virgin olive oil
- ½ cup diced red onion
- ¾ cup chopped fresh tomatoes
- ¼ tsp freshly ground black pepper
- 1 (425g) can cannellini or great northern beans, drained and rinsed
- ¼ cup finely chopped fresh curly parsley
- ½ cup Lemony Garlic Hummus
- Romaine lettuce leaves

Instructions:

1. Using a large saucepan, heat the oil. Stir in the onions, tomatoes, and pepper, and cook for 4 minutes.
2. Add the beans and cook for three more minutes, stirring occasionally. Remove from the heat, and mix in the parsley.
3. Spread 1 tbsp of hummus over each lettuce leaf. Evenly spread the warm bean mixture down the center of each leaf.
4. Fold one side of the lettuce leaf over the filling lengthwise, then fold over the other side to make a wrap and serve.

Nutritional Facts (Per Serving): Calories: 211 | Fat: 8g | Carbs: 28g | Fiber: | Protein: 10g

Chicken Edamame Salad

Prep: 10 minutes | Cook: 20 minutes | Serves 4

Ingredients:

- ⅓ cup uncooked quinoa
- 1 cup frozen shelled edamame
- 450g shredded cabbage
- ¾ cup sliced spring onions
- 2 cups cooked, shredded chicken
- 1 apple, diced
- ⅓ cup roasted cashews, chopped

For the Chili Yogurt Dressing:

- ½ cup plain Greek yogurt
- ¼ cup sweet chili sauce
- 1 tbsp toasted sesame oil
- 2 tbsp soy sauce
- ⅓ cup apple cider vinegar

Instructions:

1. Cook the quinoa as it says on the package and refrigerate after.
2. Prepare the edamame as directed on the package as well.
3. While the quinoa cooks, shred the cabbage, slice the spring onions, shred the chicken, and dice the apple.

4. Whisk the yogurt, sweet chili sauce, soy sauce, sesame oil, and vinegar in a small bowl until smooth.
5. Using a larger bowl, mix the cabbage, quinoa, edamame, chicken, cashews, apple, and spring onions.
6. Pour over the dressing, toss everything together, and serve.

Nutritional Facts (Per Serving): Calories: 381 | Fat: 13.6g | Carbs: 31.5g | Fiber: 6g | Protein: 28.9g

Leafy Lacinato Tuscan Treat

Prep: 10 minutes | Cook: 0 minutes | Serves 1

Ingredients:

- 1-tsp Dijon mustard
- 1-tbsp light mayonnaise
- 3-pcs medium-sized Lacinato kale leaves
- 1 cup grated Parmesan cheese
- 85g cooked chicken breast, thinly sliced
- 6-bulbs red onion, thinly sliced
- 1-pc apple, cut into 9-slices

Instructions:

1. Combine the mustard and mayonnaise in a small mixing bowl. Mix well until fully combined.
2. Spread the mixture generously on each of the kale leaves. Top each leaf with chicken slices, 3 apple slices, and 2 red onion slices. Roll each kale leaf into a wrap.

Nutritional Facts (Per Serving): Calories: 370 | Fat: 14g | Carbs: 29g | Fiber: | Protein: 29g

Feta & Black Bean Salad

Prep: 20 minutes | Cook: 0 minutes | Serves 4

Ingredients:

- 1 Red Onion, Sliced
- Lemons, Juiced
- 410g Black Beans, Drained
- Roma Tomatoes, Chopped
- Sea Salt to Taste
- ½ Cup Feta Cheese, Crumbled
- Olive Oil
- ½ cup Dill, Fresh & Chopped

Instructions:

1. Combine all ingredients except for the salt and feta together, and mix well.
2. Top the black bean salad with feta and salt to serve.

Nutritional Facts (Per Serving): Calories: 502 | Fat: 27g | Carbs: 72g | Fiber: 25g | Protein: 27g

Goat Cheese and Red Beans Salad

Prep: 10 minutes | Cook: 0 minutes | Serves 6

Ingredients:

- 3 cans of Red Kidney Beans, drained and rinsed well
- Water or vegetable broth to cover beans
- 1 bunch parsley, chopped
- 1½ cups red grape tomatoes, halved3 cloves garlic, minced
- Olive oil
- Lemon juice
- ½ tsp salt
- ½ tsp white pepper
- 142g goat cheese, crumbled

Instructions:

1. In a large bowl, combine beans, parsley, tomatoes, and garlic.
2. Add olive oil, lemon juice, salt, and pepper.
3. Mix well and refrigerate until ready to serve.
4. Spoon into individual dishes topped with crumbled goat cheese.

Nutritional Facts (Per Serving): Calories: 385 | Fat: 15g | Carbs: 44g | Fiber: | Protein: 22g

15-Minute Mediterranean Sardine Salad

Prep: 15 minutes | Cook: 0 minutes | Serves 4

Ingredients:

- 1 can white beans
- 2 cans sardines (127g) cans in olive oil

- 1 cup cherry tomatoes (halved)
- Green onions (chopped)
- 1 to 2 jalapenos
- 1 cup fresh Italian parsley (chopped)
- For the Dressing:
- tsp Dijon mustard
- 1 lime (zested and juiced)
- 1 to 2 garlic cloves (minced)
- 1 tsp sumac
- 1 to 2 tsp Aleppo pepper flakes

Instructions:

1. Whisk the mustard, lime zest and juice, garlic, sumac, Aleppo, and kosher salt, and black pepper in a small mixing bowl vigorously whilst drizzling in 1/3 cup extra-virgin olive oil.
2. Combine the beans, sardines, tomatoes, onions, jalapenos, and parsley and toss.
3. Pour the dressing on the salad and mix.
4. Adjust seasoning as preferred.

Nutritional Facts (Per Serving): Calories: 240 | Fat: 8g | Carbs: 21g | Fiber: 6g | Protein: 23g

Tomato Slices with Feta Cheese and Fresh Herbs

Prep: 15 minutes | Cook: 0 minutes | Serves 6

Ingredients:

- 8 large tomatoes
- 226g feta
- ¼ cup fresh parsley, chopped
- ¼ cup fresh oregano, chopped
- ½ cup Extra-virgin olive oil
- Salt and pepper, to taste

Instructions:

1. Slice tomatoes into ¼" rounds. Slice feta into the same number of thin slices.
2. Mix parsley and oregano in a bowl with olive oil. Salt and pepper, to taste.
3. Place a slice of feta on top of each tomato and spoon on herb and oil mixture. Repeat for all tomato slices.

Nutritional Facts (Per Serving): Calories: 276 | Fat: 26g | Carbs: 5g | Fiber: 2g | Protein: 6g

Lentil and Tomato Collard Wrap

Prep: 10 minutes | Cook: 10 minutes | Serves 8

Ingredients:

- (425g) cans black-eyed peas, undrained
- 1 cup baby spinach
- 1 cup chopped fresh mint
- ½ red onion, finely chopped
- 1 carrot, grated
- scallions, thinly sliced
- ½ cup extra-virgin olive oil
- 1 tbsp. white wine vinegar
- Salt
- 1/2 tsp. Freshly ground black pepper

Instructions:

1. In a large saucepan, bring the black-eyed peas and their liquid to a boil over medium heat. Cook for about 5 minutes, until heated through. Drain.
2. Return the beans to the saucepan and stir in the spinach, mint, red onion, carrot, and scallions. Heat until warmed through.
3. In a small bowl, whisk the olive oil, vinegar, salt, and pepper. Pour the mixture over the beans and stir to combine.

Nutritional Facts (Per Serving): Calories: 304 | Fat: 14g | Carbs: 33g | Fiber: 13g | Protein: 12g

MEDITERRANEAN DESSERTS RECIPES

Blueberry Cake

Prep: 5 minutes | Cook: 30 minutes | Serves 6

Ingredients:

- 2 cups almond flour
- 3 cups blueberries
- 1 cup walnuts, chopped
- 3 tbsp stevia
- 1 tsp vanilla extract
- 2 eggs, whisked
- 2 tbsp avocado oil
- 1 tsp baking powder
- Cooking spray

Instructions:

1. In a bowl, combine the flour with the blueberries, walnuts, and the other ingredients except for the cooking spray, and stir well.
2. Grease a cake pan with the cooking spray, pour the cake mix inside, introduce everything in the oven at 190°C, and bake for 30 minutes.
3. Cool the cake down, slice, and serve.

Nutritional Facts (Per Serving): Calories: 225 | Fat: 9g | Carbs: 10g | Fiber: 5g | Protein: 5g

Blackberry and Apple Cobbler

Prep: 10 minutes | Cook: 30 minutes | Serves 6

Ingredients:

- ¾ cup stevia
- 6 cups blackberries
- ¼ cup apples, cored and cubed
- ¼ tsp baking powder
- 1 tbsp lime juice
- ½ cup almond flour
- ½ cup of water
- 3½ tbsp avocado oil
- Cooking spray

Instructions:

1. In a bowl, mix the berries with half of the stevia and lemon juice, sprinkle some flour, whisk, and pour into a baking dish greased with cooking spray.
2. In another bowl, mix flour with the rest of the sugar, baking powder, the

water, and the oil, and stir the whole thing with your hands.

3. Spread over the berries, introduce in the oven at 190°C and bake for 30 minutes.
4. Serve warm.

Nutritional Facts (per Serving): Calories: 221 | Fat: 6g | Carbs: 6g | Fiber: 3g | Protein: 9g

Orange and Apricots Cake

Prep: 10 minutes | Cook: 20 minutes | Serves 8

Ingredients:

- ¾ cup stevia
- 2 cups almond flour
- ¼ cup olive oil
- ½ cup almond milk
- 1 tsp baking powder
- 2 eggs
- ½ tsp vanilla extract
- Juice and zest of 2 oranges
- 2 cups apricots, chopped

Instructions:

1. In a bowl, mix the stevia with the flour and the rest of the ingredients, whisk, and pour into a cake pan lined with parchment paper.
2. Introduce in the oven at 190°C, bake for 20 minutes, cool down, slice, and serve.

Nutritional Facts (Per Serving): Calories: 221 | Fat: 8g | Carbs: 14g | Fiber: 3g | Protein: 5g

Blueberry Yogurt Mousse

Prep: 30 minutes | Cook: 0 minutes | Serves 4

Ingredients:

- 2 cups Greek yogurt
- ¼ cup stevia
- ¾ cup heavy cream
- 2 cups blueberries

Instructions:

- In a blender, combine the yogurt with the other ingredients, pulse well, divide into cups, and keep in the fridge for 30 minutes before serving.

Nutritional Facts (Per Serving): Calories: 141 | Fat: 5g | Carbs: 8g | Fiber: 5g | Protein: 1g

Loukoumades (Fried Honey Balls)

Prep: 10 minutes | Cook: 35 minutes | Serves 10

Ingredients:

- 2 cups of sugar
- 1 cup of water
- 1 cup honey
- 1 ½ cups tepid water
- 1 tbsp. brown sugar
- ¼ cup of vegetable oil
- 1 tbsp. active dry yeast
- 1½ cups all-purpose flour,
- 1 cup cornstarch,
- ½ tsp salt
- Vegetable oil for frying
- 1 ½ cups chopped walnuts
- ¼ cup ground cinnamon

Instructions:

1. Boil the sugar and water on medium heat. Add honey after 10 minutes. cool and set aside.
2. Mix the tepid water, oil, brown sugar, and yeast in a large bowl. Allow it to sit for 10 minutes.
3. In another bowl, mix the flour, salt, and cornstarch. With your hands, mix the yeast and the flour to make a wet dough. Cover and set aside for 2 hours.
4. Fry in oil at 175°C. Measure the sizes of the dough using your palm as they are dropped in the frying pan. Fry each batch for about 3-4 minutes.
5. Immediately the loukoumades are done frying, drop them in the prepared syrup.
6. Serve with cinnamon and walnuts.

Nutritional Facts (Per Serving): Calories: 355 | Fat: 7g | Carbs: 64g | Protein: 6g

Cottage Cheese Mousse & Berries

Prep: 5 minutes | Cook: 10 minutes | Serves 3

Ingredients:

- 1 Tbsp Honey, Raw
- ½ Cup Raspberries, Fresh
- ½ Cup Blackberries, Fresh
- 249g Cottage Cheese, Soft

Instructions:

1. Start by washing your berries, and then place them in a saucepan with

your honey. Simmer for ten minutes, and then allow it to cool.
2. Lay your boiled berries in ice cream bowls, then beat your cottage cheese until it becomes a dense mouse.
3. Layer your berries and mousse together before serving.

Nutritional Facts (Per Serving): Calories: 260 | Fat: 6g | Carbs: 25g | Fiber: 6g | Protein: 23g

Almond Peaches Mix

Prep: 10 minutes | Cook: 10 minutes | Serves 4

Ingredients:

- 1/3 cup almonds, toasted
- 1/3 cup pistachios, toasted
- 1 tsp mint, chopped
- ½ cup of coconut water
- 1 tsp lemon zest, grated
- 4 peaches, halved
- 2 tbsp stevia

Instructions:

1 In a pan, combine the peaches with the stevia, and the rest of the ingredients, simmer over medium heat for 10 minutes, divide into bowls, and serve cold.

Nutritional Facts (Per Serving): Calories: 135 | Fat: 4g | Carbs: 4g | Fiber: 4g | Protein: 2g

Cocoa Brownies

Prep: 10 minutes | Cook: 20 minutes | Serves 8

Ingredients:

- 850g canned lentils, rinsed and drained
- 1 tbsp honey
- 1 banana, peeled and chopped
- ½ tsp baking soda
- 4 tbsp almond butter
- 2 tbsp cocoa powder
- Cooking spray

Instructions:

2 In a food processor, combine the lentils with the honey and the other ingredients except for the cooking spray and pulse well.

3. Pour this into a pan greased with cooking spray, spread evenly, introduce in the oven at 375 degrees F and bake for 20 minutes.
4. Cut the brownies and serve cold.

Nutritional Facts (Per Serving): Calories: 200 | Fat: 5g | Carbs: 9g | Fiber: 2g | Protein: 4g

Mixed Berries Stew

Prep: 10 minutes | Cook: 15 minutes | Serves 6

Ingredients:

- Zest of 1 lemon, grated
- Juice of 1 lemon
- ½ pint blueberries
- 1-pint strawberries halved
- 2 cups of water
- 2 tbsp stevia

Instructions:

1. In a pan, combine the berries with the water, stevia, and the other ingredients, bring to a simmer, cook over medium heat for 15 minutes, divide into bowls, and serve cold.

Nutritional Facts (Per Serving): Calories: 172 | Fat: 7g | Carbs: 8g | Fiber: 3g | Protein: 2g

Almond and Oats Pudding

Prep: 10 minutes | Cook: 15 minutes: | Serves 4

Ingredients:

- 1 tbsp lemon juice
- Zest of 1 lime
- 1 and ½ cups of almond milk
- 1 tsp almond extract
- ½ cup oats
- 2 tbsp stevia
- ½ cup silver almonds, chopped

Directions:

2. In a pan, combine the almond milk with the lime zest and the other ingredients, whisk, bring to a simmer, and cook over medium heat for 15 minutes.
3. Divide the mix into bowls and serve cold.

Nutritional Facts (Per Serving): Calories: 174 | Fat: 12g | Carbs: 4g | Fiber: 3.2g | Protein: 5g

Banana Cinnamon Cupcakes

Prep: 10 minutes | Cook: 20 minutes | Serves 4

Ingredients:

- 4 tbsp avocado oil
- 4 eggs
- 2 tsp cinnamon powder
- 1 tsp vanilla extract
- 2 bananas, peeled and chopped
- ¾ cup almond flour
- ½ tsp baking powder
- Cooking spray

Instructions:

1. In a bowl, combine the oil with the eggs, and the other ingredients except for the cooking spray, whisk well, pour in a cupcake pan greased with the cooking spray, introduce in the oven at 175ºC, and bake for 20 minutes.
2. Cool the cupcakes down and serve.

Nutritional Facts (Per Serving): Calories: 142 | Fat: 6g | Carbs: 6g | Fiber: 4g | Protein: 2g

Creamy Mint Strawberry Mix

Prep: 5 minutes | Cook: 30 minutes | Serves 6

Ingredients:

- Cooking spray
- ¼ cup stevia
- 1 and ½ cup of almond flour
- 1 tsp baking powder
- 1 cup almond milk
- 1 egg, whisked
- 2 cups strawberries, sliced
- 1 tbsp mint, chopped
- 1 tsp lime zest, grated
- ½ cup whipping cream

Instructions:

1. In a bowl, combine the almond with the strawberries, mint, and the other ingredients except for the cooking spray, and whisk well.
2. Grease 6 ramekins with the cooking spray, pour the strawberry mix inside, introduce in the oven, and bake at 175ºC, for 30 minutes.

3. Cooldown and serve.

Nutritional Facts (Per Serving): Calories: 200 | Fat: 6g | Carbs: 7g | Fiber: 2g | Protein: 8g

Cinnamon Chickpeas Cookies

Prep: 10 minutes | Cook: 20 minutes | Serves 12

Ingredients:

- 1 cup canned chickpeas, drained, rinsed and mashed
- 2 cups almond flour
- 1 tsp cinnamon powder
- 1 tsp baking powder
- 1 cup avocado oil
- ½ cup stevia
- 1 egg, whisked
- 2 tsp almond extract
- 1 cup raisins
- 1 cup coconut, unsweetened and shredded

Instructions:

1. In a bowl, combine the chickpeas with the flour, cinnamon, and the other ingredients, and whisk well until you obtain a dough.
2. Scoop tbsp of dough on a baking sheet lined with parchment paper, introduce them in the oven at 350 degrees F and bake for 20 minutes.
3. Leave them to cool down for a few minutes and serve.

Nutritional Facts (Per Serving): Calories: 200 | Fat: 5g | Carbs: 10g | Fiber: 3g | Protein: 3g

Mango Bowls

Prep: 20 minutes | Cook: 0 minutes | Serves 4

Ingredients:

- 8 cups mango, cut into medium chunks
- ½ cup of coconut water
- ¼ cup stevia
- 1 tsp vanilla extract

Instructions:

1. In a blender, combine the mango with the rest of the ingredients, pulse well, divide into bowls, and serve cold.

Nutritional Facts (Per Serving): Calories: 122 | Fat: 4g | Carbs: 7g | Fiber: 5g | Protein: 5g

MEDITERRANEAN VEGETARIAN DISHES

Spanish Rice and Beans

Prep: 5 minutes | Cook: 25 minutes | Serves 6

Ingredients:

- Extra-virgin olive oil
- 1 large yellow onion, finely chopped
- 1 green bell pepper, cored and chopped
- Kosher salt
- garlic cloves, minced
- 1 tsp smoked or sweet paprika
- 1 tsp ground cumin
- 1/2 tsp red pepper flakes, optional
- 3 cups basmati rice or similar long-grain rice rinsed very well
- 2 (425g) cans kidney beans, drained and rinsed
- 1 (425g) can diced fire roasted tomatoes
- tbsp tomato paste
- 1/2 cups vegetable broth
- 1/3 cup sliced green olives, optional, for garnish
- 1/4 cup chopped fresh cilantro or parsley, optional, for garnish

Instructions:

1. Heat 2 tbsp Extra-virgin olive in a large pan. Mix in the chopped onion, chopped bell pepper and season with a big pinch of kosher salt. Stir this until the vegetables soften a bit.
2. Add the garlic, paprika, cumin, and red pepper flakes. Cook for about 30 more seconds.
3. Pour in the rice, seasoning it with another pinch of kosher salt. Mix then add the beans and fire roasted tomatoes. In a small bowl or liquid measuring cup, mix the tomato paste and broth together, then add it to the rice mixture.
4. Increase the heat and boil, then reduce the heat to low and simmer gently. Cover, letting the rice cook until it's tender and the liquid is fully absorbed, about 20 minutes.
5. Garnish with the olives and parsley, and serve.

Nutritional Facts (Per Serving): Calories: 487 | Fat: 6g | Carbs: 91g | Fiber: 13g | Protein: 18g

Broccoli and Lentil Cakes with Avocado

Prep: 10 minutes | Cook: 20 minutes | Serves 4

Ingredients:

- 3 cups pulsed broccoli
- 2 cups canned brown lentils, drained
- 2 eggs
- ½ cup plain flour
- ¾ cup grated mozzarella cheese
- 2 Tbsp each finely chopped mint and parsley
- Salt and pepper
- Olive oil for frying
- 1 avocado, sliced
- 4 pita pockets

Instructions:

1. Place the pulsed broccoli in a microwave-safe bowl, cover, and cook in the microwave for about 3 minutes or until the broccoli is just starting to soften
2. Place the broccoli, lentils, eggs, flour, mozzarella, herbs, salt, and pepper into a food processor and pulse until a batter forms.
3. Drizzle a little olive oil into a non-stick pan over a medium-high heat
4. Take spoonfuls of the broccoli mixture and drop them onto the hot pan, cook for a couple of minutes, turn, then cook the other side until golden
5. Slice open the pita pockets, heat, and slip a couple of avocado slices into each one, then add a few patties.

Nutritional Servings (Per Serving): Calories: 584 | Fat: 21g | Carbs: 77g | Fiber: | Protein: 31g

Healthy Basil Platter

Prep: 15 minutes | Cook: 15 minutes | Serves 4

Ingredients:

- 6 pieces of red pepper cut into chunks
- 2 pieces of red onion cut into wedges
- 2 mild red chilies, diced and seeded
- Coarsely chopped garlic cloves
- 1 tsp of golden caster sugar
- 2 tbsp olive oil

- 907g small ripe tomatoes quartered up
- 340g dried pasta
- Just a handful of basil leaves
- 2 tbsp of grated Parmesan

Instructions:

1. Preheat the oven to 392 degrees Fahrenheit.
2. Take a large-sized roasting tin and scatter pepper, red onion, garlic, and chilies.
3. Sprinkle sugar on top.
4. Drizzle olive oil and season with pepper and salt.
5. Roast the veggies in your oven for 15 minutes.
6. Take a large-sized pan and cook the pasta in boiling, salted water until Al Dente.
7. Drain them.
8. Remove the veggies from the oven and tip the pasta into the veggies.
9. Toss well and tear basil leaves on top.
10. Sprinkle Parmesan and enjoy!

Nutritional Facts (Per Serving): Calories: 123 | Fat: 4g | Carbs: 10g | Protein: 2g

Onion Pakora

Prep: 10 minutes | Cook: 6 minutes | Serves 6

Ingredients:

- 1 cup graham flour
- ¼ tsp turmeric powder
- Salt to taste
- 1/8 tsp chili powder
- ¼ tsp carom
- 1 tbsp fresh coriander, chopped
- 2 green chili peppers, finely chopped
- 4 onions, finely chopped
- 2 tsp vegetable oil
- ¼ cup of rice flour

Instructions:

1. Mix the flour, water and oil in a mixing bowl and create a dough-like consistency.
2. Add peppers, onions, coriander, carom, chili powder, and turmeric.
3. Preheat the air fryer to 175°C.
4. Roll vegetable mixture into small balls, place into to the fryer and cook

for about 6-minutes. Serve with hot sauce!

Nutritional Facts (Per Serving): Calories: 253 | Fat: 12g | Carbs: 12g | Protein: 7g

Farinata

Prep: 5 minutes | Cook: 20 minutes | Serves 10

- 2 scant cups chickpea flour
- 1 tsp fine sea salt
- 1/2 cups water
- 1/4 cup extra-virgin olive oil
- 1 tsp minced fresh rosemary,
- ½ sweet yellow onion, thinly sliced
- Flaky sea salt
- Freshly ground black pepper (optional)

Instructions:

1. Whisk the chickpea flour and fine sea salt in a bowl. Follow in with water, pouring slowly and whisking constantly to avoid lumps. Let the batter sit 4 hours. Whisk in intervals, spooning off any foam that rises to the surface.
2. Turn the oven to its highest setting, just below broil.
3. Put a 14-inch pizza pan in the oven for 10 minutes. Give the batter a final whisk.
4. Take the hot skillet out of the oven, setting it on the stovetop or a heat-proof surface. Pour in the olive oil.
5. Slowly pour the batter over the back of the spoon in a steady stream.
6. Cover the surface of the batter, scooping the oil.
7. Carefully place the pizza pan on the bottom shelf of the oven. Bake for 15 to 20 minutes, until the farinata begins to turn pale gold on top. Then, switch the oven settings to "Broil."
8. Remove as the surface of the farinata turns golden-brown.
9. Take out of the oven, sprinkling flaky sea salt and freshly ground pepper.

Nutritional Facts (Per Serving): Calories: 142 | Fat: 5g | Carbs: 14g | Fiber: 3g | Protein: 5g

Curried Cashews

Prep: 5 minutes | Cook: 30 minutes | Serves 6

Ingredients:

- 6 tbsp lemon juice
- 6 tbsp curry powder
- 4 tsp kosher salt
- 6 cups unsalted cashews

Instructions:

1. Place some racks in the oven and preheat to 120°C.
2. Whisk lemon juice, curry powder, and salt in a large bowl. Add cashews. Divide between 2 large-rimmed baking sheets; spread in an even layer.
3. Bake, stirring every 15 minutes, until dry, about 45 minutes. Let cool completely. Store in an airtight container.

Nutritional Facts (Per Serving): Calories: 101 | Fat: 8g | Carbs: 6g | Protein: 3g

Batata Harra

Prep: 10 minutes | Cook: 15 minutes | Serves 4

Ingredients:

- 2 large potatoes, peeled and cut into ½ inch cubes
- Extra virgin olive oil for frying
- 2 tbsp olive oil
- 2 cloves garlic, peeled and minced
- 1 tbsp paprika
- 1 tbsp tomato paste
- ¼ tsp chili powder
- 1 handful fresh cilantro, chopped
- ¼ tbsp salt

Instructions:

1. Heat some olive oil in a frying pan to 177°C.
2. Fry the peeled potatoes for 3-5 minutes until they are golden and crispy.
3. Move the potatoes to a plate lined with paper towels to drain excess oil.
4. Using another large frying pan, heat the olive oil and sauté the garlic until golden.
5. Mix in the fried potatoes, paprika, tomato paste, and chili powder.
6. Stir until the potatoes are evenly coated with the spices.
7. Take off the heat, and drizzle in the cilantro and salt.
8. Enjoy the potatoes warm.

Nutritional Facts (Per Serving): Calories: 334 | Fat: 21g | Carbs: 35g | Fiber: 5g | Protein: 4g

Cranberry-Almond Balls

Prep: 5 minutes | Cook: 30 minutes | Serves 8

Ingredients:

- ¾ cup raw whole almonds
- ½ cup sweetened dried cranberries
- ¼ cup pitted dates
- ¾ cup old-fashioned rolled oats
- 2 tbsp tahini
- 2 tbsp fresh lemon juice
- 1 tbsp pure maple syrup

Instructions:

1. Add almonds, cranberries, and dates to a large food processor; process on High until the ingredients are broken into smaller pieces, 10 to 15 seconds.
2. Add oats, tahini, lemon juice, and maple syrup. Continue processing until a thick paste forms, 40 to 60 seconds.
3. With your hands, roll the mixture into 25 balls, about 1 tbsp per ball.

Nutritional Facts (Per Serving): Calories: 170 | Fat: 8g | Carbs: 22g | Fiber: 4g | Protein: 4g

MEDITERRANEAN MEAT RECIPES

Grilled Turmeric Chicken

Prep: 5 minutes | Cook: 15 minutes | Serves 8

Ingredients:

- 8 boneless skinless chicken thighs
- 2 lemons, juiced
- ½ cup Extra-virgin olive oil
- 2 tsp ground turmeric
- ¼ tsp ground ginger
- ¼ tsp cumin
- ¼ tsp smoked paprika
- 4 cloves fresh garlic, chopped
- ½ tbsp dried oregano
- ½ tbsp dried dill
- ½ tsp salt
- ½ tsp black pepper

Instructions:

1. Mix chicken with the rest of ingredients in a large bowl. Marinate this for at least 30 minutes but up to overnight.
2. Heat the grill and place thighs on it for 7 minutes per side.
3. Take off the grill and serve

Nutritional Facts (Per Serving): Calories: 276 | Fat: 14g | Carbs: 4g | Fiber: 14g | Protein: 33g

Grilled Chicken and Hummus in Pita

Prep: 15 minutes | Cook: 20 minutes | Serves 8

Ingredients:

- 794g Skinless boneless chicken thighs, cut into 1-inch chunks
- ¼ cup Olive oil, optional
- ¼ tsp ground black pepper
- 2 tsp Sweet paprika
- ½ tbsp Kosher salt
- 1 tsp Garlic powder
- 1 tsp Onion powder
- 1 tsp Coriander seeds
- 1 tsp Brown sugar

- ¼ tsp Cayenne pepper
- 8 Pitas
- 4 tbsp Hummus
- 4 Portions of pickled cabbage, salad, or pickles
- 6 tsp Tahini sauce

Instructions:

1. Crush the peppercorns, paprika, salt, onion powder, coriander seeds, garlic powder brown sugar, and cayenne pepper using a mortar to create a fine consistency.
2. Mix 3 tbsp of spice mix with the olive oil, and brush the mixture over the chicken pieces.
3. Skewer the marinated chicken pieces.
4. Arrange the skewers on the hot grill and turning them over every couple of minutes so that they cook evenly on all sides. The total cooking time should take 10 to 15 minutes.
5. Brown the pita bread on the grill for 1 to 2 minutes, turning them over halfway.
6. Carefully remove the pita and spread about 1 tbsp of hummus inside each one, then add a couple of tbsp of the pickled cabbage. Use a fork to carefully push the pargiyot off the skewer and into the pita.
7. Drizzle the chicken with some tahini sauce and serve.

Nutritional Facts (Per Serving): Calories: 395 | Fat: 16g | Carbs: 37g | Fiber: 3g | Protein: 27g

Yogurt-Marinated Chicken

Prep: 10 minutes | Cook: 30 minutes | Serves 6

Ingredients:

- 1 whole chicken (1.8kg) divided into pieces
- 1½ cups plain whole milk yogurt
- 2 lemons, one zested and both juiced
- 1/4 cup Extra-virgin olive oil
- garlic cloves, minced
- 2 tsp dried oregano
- 4 tsp dried mint
- 1 tsp ground cumin
- 1 tsp ground coriander
- 1 tsp sweet Spanish paprika
- 1/2 tsp freshly grated nutmeg
- 1/2 tsp freshly ground black pepper
- Kosher salt

Instructions:

1. Whisk the yogurt, lemon zest and lemon juice, olive oil, garlic, oregano, mint, cumin, coriander, paprika, nutmeg, salt and black pepper.
2. Place the chicken in the bowl with the yogurt marinade and move it around, making sure to lift the skin to coat the chicken very well. Let this sit for some hours.
3. Position a rack in the middle of the oven and heat the oven to 130°C.
4. Shake or scrape off excess marinade from each piece of chicken and arrange them on the prepared pan. Roast until chicken is cooked and somewhat browned, about 35 to 40 minutes.
5. Finish and serve.

Nutritional Facts (Per Serving): Calories: 415 | Fat: 31g | Carbs: 9g | Fiber: 2g | Protein: 27g

Spiced Lamb Chops

Prep: 10 minutes | Cook: 15 minutes | Serves 8

Ingredients:

- 1 Tbsp Mint, Fresh & Chopped
- 1 Tsp Garlic Paste
- 1 Tsp Allspice
- ½ Tsp Nutmeg
- ½ Tsp Green Cardamom
- ¼ Tsp Hot Paprika
- Sea Salt & Black Pepper to Taste
- 4 Tbsp Olive Oil
- 4 Tbsp Lemon Juice, Fresh
- 2 Racks of Lamb Chops, Trimmed & Separated into 16 Chops

Instructions:

1. Start by getting out a large bowl and mixing all your ingredients except for your lamb chops. Mix well, and then coat the chops in the mixture.
2. Marinate for five to six hours, then preheat your grill to high heat.
3. Grease your grill grates, then grill the chops for seven minutes. Flip halfway through, and serve hot.

Nutritional Facts (Per Serving): Calories: 500 | Fat: 31g | Carbs: 3g | Fiber: 1g | Protein: 38g

Chicken in a Caper Sauce

Prep: 10 minutes | Cook: 20 minutes | Serves 2

Ingredients:

- ½ Cup All Purpose Flour
- Sea Salt to Taste
- 2 Chicken Breast Halves, Boneless & Skinless
- 2 Tbsp Olive Oil
- ¼ Cup Dry White Wine
- ¼ Cup Unsalted Butter, Cold & Cubed
- 3 Tbsp Lime Juice, Fresh
- 2 Tbsp Capers, Drained
- ½ Lime, Sliced into Wedges

Instructions:

1. Mix some salt and flour, and chicken breasts thoroughly well.
2. Shake off any excess flour, and fry in heated olive oil, four minutes per side.
3. Move onto a plate
4. Move in your wine to deglaze the pan. Bring it to a boil, scraping any browned bits from the bottom.
5. Add the lemon juice in, cooking for three minutes more.
6. Add in your butter, and cook until your sauce thickens. Make sure the sauce doesn't stick and burn.
7. Remove the sauce from heat, and then add in your capers. Stir to mix well, and place this sauce over your chicken to serve warm.

Nutritional Facts (Per Serving): Calories: 520 | Fat: 38g | Carbs: 3g | Fiber: 1g | Protein: 39g

Ground Turkey Skillet Dinner with Spinach, Tomatoes, White Beans and Homemade Croutons

Ingredients:

- Extra-virgin olive oil
- 1 1/2 tsp Kosher salt
- Freshly ground pepper
- 4 cups 1-inch cube crusty bread
- 1 medium yellow onion
- cloves garlic, minced
- 454g lean ground turkey
- 1 tsp ground fennel

- 1 tsp oregano
- ½ tsp thyme
- ½ tsp Aleppo pepper or red pepper flakes
- 1 pint grape tomatoes
- 2 to 3 handfuls baby spinach
- 1 roasted red pepper, roughly chopped
- 1 (439g) can cannellini beans, drained and rinsed
- Kosher salt
- freshly ground pepper
- 2 tbsp red wine vinegar

Instructions:

1. Heat two tbsp of oil in a large skillet and put in the bread cubes, 1 tsp salt and pepper. Toast this, stirring until lightly browned and crisp, 4 minutes.
2. Place the croutons on a plate.
3. Pour one tbsp of olive oil into the same pan. Add the onion, and sauté this for 5 minutes.
4. Add the garlic, ground turkey, fennel, oregano, thyme, Aleppo pepper, Kosher salt, and freshly ground black pepper.
5. Cut the turkey into smaller sizes. Add the cherry tomatoes. Cook for 15 minutes until the ground turkey browns and the tomatoes burst and blister.
6. Add the chopped roasted red peppers, spinach, beans. Stir until everything is combined, warmed through and the spinach has wilted. Add the vinegar and croutons. Stir to combine.
7. Enjoy.

Nutritional Facts (Per Serving): Calories: 364 | Fat: 14g | Carbs: 29g | Fiber: 3.2g | Protein: 33g

MEDITERRANEAN FISH AND SEAFOOD DISHES

Pan Seared Shrimp with Lemon-Garlic Braised Greens

Prep: 15 minutes | Cook: 25 minutes | Serves 4

Ingredients:

- 680g jumbo shrimp, peeled and deveined
- Extra-virgin olive oil
- 4 garlic cloves, chopped
- 1/4 tsp crushed red pepper flakes
- 1/2 tsp sea salt
- 1/4 tsp freshly ground black pepper
- 1 lemon, zested
- 453g mixed cooking greens (Swiss chard, kale, dandelion, and/or spinach)
- 1/4 cup Extra-virgin olive oil
- 4 garlic cloves, sliced
- 1/2 tsp sea salt
- 1/4 tsp freshly ground pepper
- Crushed red pepper flakes
- 1 1/2 cups warm water
- 1 lemon, juiced
- 1/4 cup chopped fresh parsley
- Lemon wedges

Instructions:

1. Whisk the shrimp and whisk ¼ cup Extra-virgin olive oil, garlic, red pepper flakes, sea salt, freshly ground pepper, and lemon zest.
2. Rinse and drain the greens thoroughly, removing the tough stems and roughly chopping the leaves.
3. Place a skillet on medium-high heat, with enough olive oil coating the bottom.
4. Pour in the sliced garlic and cook for about 30 seconds, just until fragrant.
5. Follow up with half of the mixed greens and cook for two minutes,
6. As the greens wilt, add the remaining greens and cook for 3 minutes more, stirring continuously.
7. Season the greens with salt, pepper, and crushed red pepper. Add water, let it boil, then reduce to a simmer for 10 minutes until the water has evaporated.
8. Turn off the heat and stir in the lemon juice.
9. Drizzle some oil and add the shrimp and all of the marinade. Cook for 2 to 3 minutes on each side.
10. Serve the greens on a warmed platter with the cooked shrimp and any sauce from the pan.

Nutritional Facts (Per Serving): Calories: 298 | Fat: 17g | Carbs: 11g | Fiber: 6g | Protein: 27g

Shrimp Scampi

- 1 (227g) package angel hair pasta
- ½ cup butter, or to taste
- 1 pound shrimp, peeled and deveined
- cloves minced garlic
- 1 cup dry white wine
- ¼ tsp ground black pepper
- ¾ cup grated Parmesan cheese
- 1 tbsp chopped fresh parsley
- lemon wedges

Instructions

- Bring a large pot of lightly salted water to a boil. Cook pasta in the boiling water, stirring occasionally, until tender yet firm to the bite, 4 to 5 minutes. Drain; transfer pasta to a serving bowl and keep warm.
- Melt butter in a large saucepan over medium heat. Stir in shrimp and garlic; cook and stir until shrimp turns pink, 3 to 5 minutes.
- Stir in white wine and pepper; bring to a boil. Cook and stir for 30 seconds.
- Pour shrimp with sauce over pasta in the serving bowl; toss well. Sprinkle with Parmesan cheese and parsley.
- Serve with lemon wedges.

Nutritional Facts (Per Serving): Calories: 635 | Fat: 32g | Carbs: 45g | Fiber: 2g | Protein: 35g

Tilapia & Capers

Prep: 10 minutes | Cook: 20 minutes | Serves 4

Ingredients:

- 1 ½ Tbsp Butter, Melted
- 453g Tilapia, Chopped into 8 Pieces
- ¼ Cup Capers
- Tbsp Lemon Juice, Fresh
- Cloves Garlic, Minced
- Shallots, Chopped
- Fine Sea Salt & Black Pepper to Taste
- 1½ Tsp Paprika
- 1½ Tsp Cumin

Instructions:

1. Start by heating your oven to 190, then get a baking sheet. Grease the baking sheet and place it to the side.
2. Get out a small bowl and mix your paprika, salt, pepper, and cumin.
3. In another bowl, mix your garlic, lemon juice, butter, and shallots until combined.
4. Season your tilapia using the spice mixture and butter mixture.
5. Arrange the fillets on the baking sheet, topping with capers. Cook for ten to fifteen minutes. Your fillets should be cooked through and flaked easily with a fork. Serve warm.

Nutritional Facts (Per Serving): Calories: 210 | Fat: 9g | Carbs: 3g | Fiber: 1g | Protein: 26g

Italian Seafood Risotto with Saffron and Prawns

Prep: 5 minutes | Cook: 25 minutes | Serves 2

Ingredients:

- Arborio rice
- 12 large shrimps, peeled and deveined
- 1 small onion, chopped
- 3 cloves garlic
- ¼ tsp saffron threads
- Dry wine
- Fish or Seafood broth
- 2 tbsp butter
- 2 tbsp olive oil
- Salt and pepper to taste
- Fresh parsley
- Grated Parmesan cheese

Instructions:

1. Pour some dry white wine into a small bowl and soak the saffron threads.
2. Heat a tbsp of butter and olive oil in a saucepan and sauté the chopped onions till translucent.
3. Add in the minced garlic and the Arborio rice. Stir this for 2 minutes until the rice is lightly toasted.
4. Pour in the saffron-infused wine and cook until the liquid is largely absorbed.
5. Boil the fish/seafood broth and add it gradually into the rice, stirring until the it is absorbed into the rice each time. Continue until the rice is creamy and al dente
6. Melt a tbsp of butter in a different pan and fry the prawns until they're cooked through.
7. Fold the pawns into the risotto and season with salt and pepper.
8. Serve the seafood risotto with grated parmesan cheese.

Nutritional Facts (Pe Serving): Calories: 530 | Fat: 20g | Carbs: 59g | Fiber: 2g | Protein: 24g

Stewed Squid

Prep: 5 minutes | Cook: 10 minutes | Serves 2

Ingredients:

- 1 Tbsp Olive Oil
- Fresh Parsley
- Sea Salt
- 1 Onion
- 2 Squids

Instructions:

- Start by chopping your onions into thin rings.
- Place a skillet over medium heat, and then heat your oil. Once it's hot, fry the onion until they turn translucent.
- Add in your onions, and season with salt. Allow it to simmer for three minutes, and then serve with chopped parsley.

Nutritional Facts (Per Serving): Calories: 150 | Fat: 7g | Carbs: 6g | Fiber: 2g | Protein: 22g

Trout & Wilted Greens

Prep: 5 minutes | Cook: 15 minutes | Serves 4

Ingredients:

- 1 Lemon, Juiced & Zested
- Sea Salt & Black Pepper to Taste
- Trout Fillets, 142g Each, Boneless & Skinless
- ½ Sweet Onion, Sliced Thin
- 2 Cups Swiss Chard, Chopped
- 4 Cups Kale, Chopped
- 2 Tsp Olive Oil

Instructions:

1. Start by heating your oven to 170°C, then grease a nine-by-thirteen-inch baking dish.
2. Place your onion, kale and Swiss chard in the dish, and top with the fish.
3. The skin side should be up. Drizzle with lemon juice and oil. Season with salt and pepper before baking for fifteen minutes.

4 Sprinkle with lemon zest before serving.

60-DAYS MEDITERRANEAN DIET MEAL PLAN

Day	Breakfast	Lunch	Snack	Dinner
1	Cauliflower Tabbouleh	Meal-Prep Falafel Bowls with Tahini Sauce	Carrot Cake Energy Bites	One-Skillet salmon with Fennel & Sun-dried Tomato Couscous
2	Date and Nut Granola with Greek Yogurt	Mediterranean Rice Pilaf	Greek Yogurt Breakfast Parfait	Padma Lakshmi's Tandoori Chicken Salad
3	Buckwheat Pancakes with Coconut Cream	Mussels with Cheese	Savory Date & Pistachio Bites	Feta & Roasted Red Pepper Stuffed Chicken Breast
4	Herb & Feta Savory Muffins	Chicken with Tomatoes, Prunes, Cinnamon, and Wine	Greek Salad on a Stick	BBQ Shrimp with Garlicky Kale & Parmesan-Herb Couscous
5	Tomato Toasts with Mint Yogurt and Sumac Vinaigrette	Mushroom risotto	Peanut Butter Energy Balls	Walnut-Rosemary Crusted Salmon
6	Tuna and White Bean Salad with Poached Eggs	Organic Mini Minty Lamb Koftas	Salmon Cakes with Potato and Fire Roasted Corn Salsa	One Pot Beef Stew
7	Pan Con Tomate	Baked Prawns with Tomatoes and Feta	Pistachio & Peach Toast	Linguine with Creamy White Clam Sauce
8	Feta and Tomato Rice	Arborio Rice and White Bean Soup	Everything-Bagel Crispy Chickpeas	Baked Haddock with Baby Bell Peppers
9	Greek Omelette with Mint and Zucchini	Grenadian Cod and Orange Salad with Olives	Muhammara (Roasted Red Pepper and Walnut Dip)	Farfalle with Tuna, Lemon and Fennel
Day	Breakfast	Lunch	Snack	Dinner
10	Mediterranean Edamame & Herb Salad	Chinese Cabbage with Mint and Green Peas	Cranberry-Almond Energy Balls	Tomato and Pepper Poached Cod

Day	Breakfast	Lunch	Snack	Dinner
11	Lebanese Breakfast Bulgur Cereal with Fruit and nuts	Greek Pasta Salad	Crunchy Sugar-Free Granola	Bean Counter Chowder
12	Mediterranean Chickpea Egg Salad	Bruschetta Chicken Pasta	Almond Crackers	Italian Seafood Risotto with Saffron and Prawns
13	Vegetable Omelet	White Bean Soup with Escarole	Rosemary-Garlic Pecans	One-Pan Chicken Parmesan Pasta
14	Mediterranean Breakfast Sandwich	One-Pot Tomato Basil Pasta	Spanakopita	Spanish Grilled Sardines with Lemon and Paprika
15	Fried Eggs with Smoked Salmon and Lemon Cream	Chicken Meatball Soup	Peanut Butter Sesame Seed Balls	Pan Seared Shrimp with Lemon-Garlic Braised Greens
16	Mediterranean Breakfast Pita	Greek Bean Soup (Fasolada)	Greek Fava	Seared Salmon with Pesto Fettuccine
17	Lemon-Dill Asparagus	Scallop Ceviche	Kalamata Olive Tapenade	Italian White Bean Soup
18	Turkish Breakfast Wrap with Sausage, Eggs and Vegetables	Grilled Turmeric Chicken	Tortilla De Patata (Spanish Potato Omelette)	Asparagus Risotto
19	Lemony Greek Chickpea Soup	Turkish Pilaf	Apple with Cinnamon Almond Butter	Chicken Adobo
20	Apricot and Almond Breakfast CousCous	Crispy Smoked Tofu & Coleslaw Wraps	Greek Stuffed Grape Leaves	Yogurt-Marinated Chicken
21	Balela Salad	Grilled Chicken and Hummus in Pita	White Corn No-Bake Balls	Seafood Ravioli in Cream Cheese Sauce
22	Avocado Toast with Caramelized Balsamic Onions	Lemon-Garlic Shrimp Pasta	Spicy Rosemary Olives	Chicken Spinach Soup with Fresh Pesto

Day	Breakfast	Lunch	Snack	Dinner

DAY	BREAKFAST	LUNCH	SNACK	DINNER
23	Spanakorizo	Summer Squash & White Bean Soup	Kale Chips	Ground Turkey Skillet Dinner with Spinach, Tomatoes, White Beans and Homemade Croutons
24	Farinata	Ben Tish's Duck and Fig Ponchos	Classic Hummus with Pita Bread	Shrimp Scampi
25	Mediterranean Chickpea and Spinach Breakfast Bowl	Salmon Rice Bowl	Tuna Deviled Eggs	Moroccan Chicken Pastilla
26	15-Minute Mediterranean Sardine Salad	Chicken Fajita Soup	Zucchini Fritters with Feta, Cheddar, Mint and Parsley	Red Lentil Soup Mix
27	Mint Tea and Olive Biscuits	Spanish rice and beans	Curried Cashews	Creamy Seafood Bisque
28	Eggs Florentine	Linguine with Sun-dried Tomatoes, Olives, and Lemon	Tomato Slices with Feta Cheese and Fresh Herbs	Tahini Chicken with Polenta
29	Busy Morning Egg Muffins	Pesto Pasta Salad	French Tuna Rilletes	Spinach Ravioli with Artichokes & Olives
30	Shakshuka	Cauliflower Rice Paella	Spanakopita	Seafood Soup
31	Parmesan & Spinach Egg Bake	Vegetable Ravioli Soup	Batata Harra	Tilapia & Capers
32	Mediterranean Chickpea Egg Salad	Feta & Black Bean Salad	Creamy Mint Strawberry Mix	Stewed squid
33	Fried Eggs with Smoked Salmon and Lemon Cream	Eggplant Stew	Tuna Deviled Eggs	Seared Salmon with Pesto Fettuccine
34	Turkish Breakfast Wrap with Sausage, Eggs and Vegetables	Bruschetta Chicken Pasta	Blueberry Cake	Yogurt-Marinated Chicken
35	Sweet Potato Hash	Maqboulleh	Kalamata Olive Tapenade	Spiced Lamb Chops

DAY	BREAKFAST	LUNCH	SNACK	DINNER
36	Blueberry Yogurt Mousse	Cannellini Bean Lettuce Wraps	Onion Pakora	Creamy Seafood Bisque
37	Date and Nut Granola with Greek Yogurt	Ben Tish's Duck and Fig Ponchos	Zucchini Fritters with Feta, Cheddar, Mint and Parsley	Risi e Bisi
38	Lemon-Dill Asparagus	Lemon-Garlic Shrimp Pasta	Tortilla De Patata (Spanish Potato Omelette)	Linguine with Creamy White Clam Sauce
39	Eggs Florentine	Organic Mini Minty Lamb Koftas	Blackberry and Apples Cobbler	Bean Counter Chowder
40	Shakshuka	Chicken Edamame Salad	Crunchy Sugar-Free Granola	Spaghetti Al Pomodoro Crudo
41	Banana Cinnamon Cupcakes	Chicken in a Caper Sauce	Mango Bowls	Pea Stew
42	Broccoli and Lentil Cakes with Avocado	Baked Prawns with Tomatoes and Feta	Cocoa Brownies	Italian Seafood Risotto with Saffron and Prawns
43	Tomato Toasts with Mint Yogurt and Sumac Vinaigrette	Vegetable Ravioli Soup	Almond Peaches Mix	BBQ Shrimp with Garlicky Kale & Parmesan-Herb Couscous
44	Sweet Potato Hash	Chinese Cabbage with Mint and Green Peas	Greek Fava	Farfalle with Tuna, Lemon and Fennel
45	Apricot and Almond Breakfast CousCous	Passion Fruit and Spicy Couscous	Cocoa Brownies	Moroccan Chicken Pastilla
46	15-Minute Mediterranean Sardine Salad	Mussels with Cheese	Almond Crackers	Risotto Carbonara
47	Greek Omelette with Mint and Zucchini	Crispy Smoked Tofu & Coleslaw Wraps	Orange and Apricots Cake	Baked Haddock with Baby Bell Peppers
48	Cottage Cheese Mousse & Berries	Leafy Lacinato Tuscan Treat	Pistachio & Peach Toast	Tomato and Pepper Poached Cod
49	Balela Salad	Grilled Turmeric Chicken	Cinnamon Chickpeas Cookies	Spiced Lamb Chops

50	Cauliflower Tabbouleh	Tomato and Cherry Linguine	Healthy Basil Platter	Tilapia & Capers
51	Herb & Feta Savory Muffins	Cauliflower Rice Paella	Zucchini Fritters with Feta, Cheddar, Mint and Parsley	Trout & Wilted Greens
52	Green Poached Eggs on Toast	Summer Squash & White Bean Soup	Cocoa Brownies	Lentil and Tomato Collard Wrap
53	Spanakorizo	Garlic & Seafood Couscous	Almond Peaches Mix	Spaghetti Al Pomodoro Crudo
54	Avocado Toast with Caramelized Balsamic Onions	Grenadian Cod and Orange Salad with Olives	Loukoumades	Padma Lakshmi's Tandoori Chicken Salad
55	Mint Tea and Olive Biscuits	Pasta with Arugula and Walnut and Pesto	Classic Hummus with Pita Bread	One-Pan Chicken Parmesan Pasta
56	Buckwheat Pancakes with Coconut Cream	Scallop Ceviche	Mixed Berries Stew	One Pot Beef Stew
57	Farinata	Goat Cheese 'n Red Beans Salad	White Corn No-Bake Balls	Shrimp Scampi
58	Mediterranean Edamame & Herb Salad	Chicken Fajita Soup	Kale Chips	Ground Turkey Skillet Dinner with Spinach, Tomatoes, White Beans and Homemade Croutons
59	Cottage Cheese Mousse & Berries	Mediterranean-Style Chicken and Rice	Greek Yogurt Breakfast Parfait	Italian White Bean Soup
60	Lebanese Breakfast Bulgur Cereal with Fruit and nuts	Jackfruit and Chilli Stew	Almond and Oats Pudding	Seafood Ravioli in Cream Cheese Sauce

Printed in Dunstable, United Kingdom